TEACHER'S PET PUBLICATIONS

PUZZLE PACK
for
Bridge to Terabithia
based on the book by
Katherine Paterson

Written by
William T. Collins

© 2005 Teacher's Pet Publications
All Rights Reserved

The materials in this packet are copyrighted
by Teacher's Pet Publications, Inc.

These pages may be duplicated by the purchaser
for use in the purchaser's own classroom.

Copying any of these materials and distributing them
for any other purpose is a violation of the copyright laws.

© 2005 Teacher's Pet Publications, Inc.
www.tpet.com

INTRODUCTION
If you already own the LitPlan for this title, this Puzzle Pack will refresh your Unit Resource Materials and Vocabulary Resource Materials sections plus give you additional materials you can substitute into the tests. If you do not already have a complete LitPlan, these pages will give you some supplemental materials to use with your own plan. There are two main groups of materials: one set for unit words (such as characters' names, symbols, places, etc.) and one set for vocabulary words associated with the book.

WORD LIST
There is a word list for both the unit words and the vocabulary words. These lists show you which words are being used in the materials and the clues or definitions being used for those words. You may want to give students a word list with clues/definitions to help them, or you may want students to only have a word list (without clues/definitions) if you want them to work a little harder. Both are available for duplication. The word lists can also be your "calling key" for the bingo games.

FILL IN THE BLANK AND MATCHING
There are 4 each of the fill in the blank and matching worksheets for both the unit and vocabulary words. These pages can be used either as extra worksheets for students or as objective parts of a unit test. They can be done individually if students need extra help or as a whole class activity to review the material covered.

MAGIC SQUARES
The magic squares not only reinforce the material covered but also work on reasoning and math skills. Many teachers have told us that their students really enjoy doing these!

WORD SEARCH PUZZLES
The word search words go in all directions, as indicated on your answer keys. Two of the word search puzzles have the clues listed rather than the words. This makes the puzzle a little more difficult, but it reinforces the material better. Two word search puzzles have words only for students who find the clue puzzles too difficult.

CROSSWORD PUZZLES
Both unit and vocabulary word sections have 4 crossword puzzles.

BINGO CARDS
There are 32 individual bingo cards for the unit words and 32 individual bingo cards for the vocabulary words. You can use your word list as a "call list," calling the words at random and marking them off of your list as you go, or you could use the flash cards by cutting them apart and drawing the words at random from a hat (or box or whatever). To make a better review, you might ask for the definition and spelling of each word as you call it out–or you could call out the definitions and have students tell you the words they need to look for on the puzzle.

JUGGLE LETTERS
The vocabulary juggle letter game is intended to help students learn the spellings of the words. One sheet has the definitions listed on it as an extra help for students who need it or to reinforce the definitions if you choose to do so.

FLASH CARDS
We've included a set of vocabulary flash cards you can duplicate, cut, and fold for your students. Some teachers make a few sets for general use by the class; others make a set for each student. Some teachers duplicate them for each student and have the students cut & fold their own. You can cut out just the words and put them in a hat, have each student pick out one word and write the definition and a sentence for that word. Students then swap words and papers, with the next student adding a sentence of his own under the last one. You can have students swap as many times as you like. Each time the student will read the sentences written prior to his own and then add a sentence. You can cut out the words and definitions separately and play "I Have; Who Has?" Each student in the room draws a word and definition. The first student says, "I have (the name of the word). Who has the definition?" The student with the definition reads it then says, "I have (the name of the vocabulary word she has). Who has the definition?" The round continues until all words and definitions have been given.

Bridge to Terabithia Word List

No.	Word	Clue/Definition
1.	ARLINGTON	Leslie's old school
2.	BARBIE	May Belle's beloved Christmas gift
3.	BEANS	Jesse needs to pick and can these
4.	BRENDA	Eighth grade Aarons daughter
5.	DRAWING	Jesse's favorite pastime
6.	DROWNED	How Leslie died
7.	EASTER	Leslie wanted to go to church with Jesse then
8.	ELLIE	Eldest Aarons daughter
9.	FIFTH	Grade Leslie and Jesse were in at Lark Creek
10.	FIRST	What Leslie calls her parents by; ---- names
11.	FREE	Miss Edmunds' favorite song; --- to Be You and Me
12.	FRIDAYS	Miss Edmunds' day at Lark Creek
13.	GEORGIA	Mrs. Aarons' homeplace
14.	GOLDEN	Refinished room of the Burke's; ____ room
15.	GUITAR	Miss Edmunds' instrument
16.	GUTS	Jesse thinks he has none
17.	JANICE	Seventh grade bully; ____ Avery
18.	JESSE	Ten-year-old boy in family of all girls
19.	JOYCE	Jesse's youngest sister; ____ Ann
20.	JUDY	Leslie's parents; ____ and Bill
21.	KING	Jesse reigned as this over their kingdom
22.	LAIDOFF	What happened to Jesse's dad (2 words)
23.	LARK	Local elementary school; ____ Creek
24.	LESLIE	Fastest runner in the fifth grade
25.	LUMBER	Used to build bridge over creek bed
26.	MAY	Worships Jesse; ____ Belle
27.	BESSIE	Jesse milks her daily; Miss ____
28.	EDMUNDS	Peace-loving music teacher; Miss ____
29.	MONSTER	Fifth grade teacher; ____ Mouth Myers
30.	NARNIA	Magical kingdom in C.S. Lewis stories
31.	GALLERY	Day trip Miss Edmunds and Jesse take; Nat'l. Art ____
32.	NEAT	What Miss Edmunds calls Jesse; ____ Kid
33.	PAINT	Christmas gift to Jesse from Leslie; ___ set
34.	DOLLS	Bribe May Belle took; paper ____
35.	PATERSON	Author
36.	PENNSYLVANIA	Where Leslie's ashes were taken
37.	FOREST	Sacred place; Pine ____
38.	TERRIEN	Guardian of Terabithia; Prince ____
39.	QUEEN	Leslie reigned as this over Terabithia
40.	RACING	Jesse's Christmas gift from his dad; ___ car set
41.	RAIN	Evil curse
42.	ROPE	Entry into secret kingdom; ____ swing
43.	SCUBA	Topic of Leslie's essay; ____ diving
44.	BLOUSE	Ellie's purchase in Millsburg; see-through ____
45.	TERABITHIA	Secret place
46.	THIRTYONE	Number of students in the fifth-grade class
47.	TV	Burke's have none
48.	UHAUL	Delivers new people to the old Perkins' place
49.	VALUE	What Leslie's parents were reassessing; ____ structure
50.	WASHINGTON	Jesse's dad drives there everyday to work; ____ D.C.
51.	WRITERS	Leslie's parents' jobs

Bridge to Terabithia Fill In The Blank 1

_____ 1. Christmas gift to Jesse from Leslie; ___ set

_____ 2. Jesse's favorite pastime

_____ 3. What Leslie calls her parents by; ---- names

_____ 4. Leslie's parents' jobs

_____ 5. Refinished room of the Burke's; ____ room

_____ 6. Grade Leslie and Jesse were in at Lark Creek

_____ 7. Leslie's parents; ____ and Bill

_____ 8. Local elementary school; ____ Creek

_____ 9. Entry into secret kingdom; ____ swing

_____ 10. Ten-year-old boy in family of all girls

_____ 11. Leslie reigned as this over Terabithia

_____ 12. Worships Jesse; ___ Belle

_____ 13. Miss Edmunds' favorite song; --- to Be You and Me

_____ 14. Jesse thinks he has none

_____ 15. Miss Edmunds' day at Lark Creek

_____ 16. Evil curse

_____ 17. What Leslie's parents were reassessing; ____ structure

_____ 18. Jesse milks her daily; Miss ____

_____ 19. Fastest runner in the fifth grade

_____ 20. Day trip Miss Edmunds and Jesse take; Nat'l. Art ____

Bridge to Terabithia Fill In The Blank 1 Answer Key

Answer	Clue
PAINT	1. Christmas gift to Jesse from Leslie; ___ set
DRAWING	2. Jesse's favorite pastime
FIRST	3. What Leslie calls her parents by; ---- names
WRITERS	4. Leslie's parents' jobs
GOLDEN	5. Refinished room of the Burke's; ____ room
FIFTH	6. Grade Leslie and Jesse were in at Lark Creek
JUDY	7. Leslie's parents; ____ and Bill
LARK	8. Local elementary school; ____ Creek
ROPE	9. Entry into secret kingdom; ____ swing
JESSE	10. Ten-year-old boy in family of all girls
QUEEN	11. Leslie reigned as this over Terabithia
MAY	12. Worships Jesse; ___ Belle
FREE	13. Miss Edmunds' favorite song; --- to Be You and Me
GUTS	14. Jesse thinks he has none
FRIDAYS	15. Miss Edmunds' day at Lark Creek
RAIN	16. Evil curse
VALUE	17. What Leslie's parents were reassessing; ____ structure
BESSIE	18. Jesse milks her daily; Miss ____
LESLIE	19. Fastest runner in the fifth grade
GALLERY	20. Day trip Miss Edmunds and Jesse take; Nat'l. Art ____

Bridge to Terabithia Fill In The Blank 2

1. Day trip Miss Edmunds and Jesse take; Nat'l. Art _____
2. Mrs. Aarons' homeplace
3. Entry into secret kingdom; _____ swing
4. Evil curse
5. Seventh grade bully; _____ Avery
6. Magical kingdom in C.S. Lewis stories
7. What Miss Edmunds calls Jesse; _____ Kid
8. Author
9. Guardian of Terabithia; Prince _____
10. Eighth grade Aarons daughter
11. Number of students in the fifth-grade class
12. Ellie's purchase in Millsburg; see-through _____
13. Delivers new people to the old Perkins' place
14. Grade Leslie and Jesse were in at Lark Creek
15. Fifth grade teacher; _____ Mouth Myers
16. Jesse's dad drives there everyday to work; _____ D.C.
17. Jesse milks her daily; Miss _____
18. Worships Jesse; ___ Belle
19. Bribe May Belle took; paper _____
20. Miss Edmunds' favorite song; --- to Be You and Me

Bridge to Terabithia Fill In The Blank 2 Answer Key

GALLERY	1. Day trip Miss Edmunds and Jesse take; Nat'l. Art ____
GEORGIA	2. Mrs. Aarons' homeplace
ROPE	3. Entry into secret kingdom; ____ swing
RAIN	4. Evil curse
JANICE	5. Seventh grade bully; ____ Avery
NARNIA	6. Magical kingdom in C.S. Lewis stories
NEAT	7. What Miss Edmunds calls Jesse; ____ Kid
PATERSON	8. Author
TERRIEN	9. Guardian of Terabithia; Prince ____
BRENDA	10. Eighth grade Aarons daughter
THIRTYONE	11. Number of students in the fifth-grade class
BLOUSE	12. Ellie's purchase in Millsburg; see-through ____
UHAUL	13. Delivers new people to the old Perkins' place
FIFTH	14. Grade Leslie and Jesse were in at Lark Creek
MONSTER	15. Fifth grade teacher; ____ Mouth Myers
WASHINGTON	16. Jesse's dad drives there everyday to work; ____ D.C.
BESSIE	17. Jesse milks her daily; Miss ____
MAY	18. Worships Jesse; ___ Belle
DOLLS	19. Bribe May Belle took; paper ____
FREE	20. Miss Edmunds' favorite song; --- to Be You and Me

Bridge to Terabithia Fill In The Blank 3

1. Ten-year-old boy in family of all girls
2. Jesse's dad drives there everyday to work; ____ D.C.
3. Jesse's youngest sister; ____ Ann
4. Leslie wanted to go to church with Jesse then
5. Where Leslie's ashes were taken
6. Jesse reigned as this over their kingdom
7. Miss Edmunds' day at Lark Creek
8. Burke's have none
9. Used to build bridge over creek bed
10. Mrs. Aarons' homeplace
11. Jesse's Christmas gift from his dad; ___ car set
12. Grade Leslie and Jesse were in at Lark Creek
13. Delivers new people to the old Perkins' place
14. Miss Edmunds' favorite song; --- to Be You and Me
15. Day trip Miss Edmunds and Jesse take; Nat'l. Art ____
16. May Belle's beloved Christmas gift
17. Seventh grade bully; ____ Avery
18. Jesse needs to pick and can these
19. Leslie's old school
20. Ellie's purchase in Millsburg; see-through _____

Bridge to Terabithia Fill In The Blank 3 Answer Key

JESSE	1. Ten-year-old boy in family of all girls
WASHINGTON	2. Jesse's dad drives there everyday to work; ____ D.C.
JOYCE	3. Jesse's youngest sister; ____ Ann
EASTER	4. Leslie wanted to go to church with Jesse then
PENNSYLVANIA	5. Where Leslie's ashes were taken
KING	6. Jesse reigned as this over their kingdom
FRIDAYS	7. Miss Edmunds' day at Lark Creek
TV	8. Burke's have none
LUMBER	9. Used to build bridge over creek bed
GEORGIA	10. Mrs. Aarons' homeplace
RACING	11. Jesse's Christmas gift from his dad; ___ car set
FIFTH	12. Grade Leslie and Jesse were in at Lark Creek
UHAUL	13. Delivers new people to the old Perkins' place
FREE	14. Miss Edmunds' favorite song; --- to Be You and Me
GALLERY	15. Day trip Miss Edmunds and Jesse take; Nat'l. Art ____
BARBIE	16. May Belle's beloved Christmas gift
JANICE	17. Seventh grade bully; ____ Avery
BEANS	18. Jesse needs to pick and can these
ARLINGTON	19. Leslie's old school
BLOUSE	20. Ellie's purchase in Millsburg; see-through _____

Bridge to Terabithia Fill In The Blank 4

_____ 1. Author

_____ 2. Ten-year-old boy in family of all girls

_____ 3. Eighth grade Aarons daughter

_____ 4. Jesse's Christmas gift from his dad; ___ car set

_____ 5. Seventh grade bully; ____ Avery

_____ 6. Evil curse

_____ 7. Guardian of Terabithia; Prince ____

_____ 8. Grade Leslie and Jesse were in at Lark Creek

_____ 9. Eldest Aarons daughter

_____ 10. Jesse's youngest sister; ____ Ann

_____ 11. Number of students in the fifth-grade class

_____ 12. Topic of Leslie's essay; ____ diving

_____ 13. Delivers new people to the old Perkins' place

_____ 14. Mrs. Aarons' homeplace

_____ 15. Local elementary school; ____ Creek

_____ 16. Fastest runner in the fifth grade

_____ 17. What Leslie calls her parents by; ---- names

_____ 18. Leslie's parents' jobs

_____ 19. Sacred place; Pine _____

_____ 20. May Belle's beloved Christmas gift

Bridge to Terabithia Fill In The Blank Answer Key

PATERSON	1. Author
JESSE	2. Ten-year-old boy in family of all girls
BRENDA	3. Eighth grade Aarons daughter
RACING	4. Jesse's Christmas gift from his dad; ___ car set
JANICE	5. Seventh grade bully; ____ Avery
RAIN	6. Evil curse
TERRIEN	7. Guardian of Terabithia; Prince ____
FIFTH	8. Grade Leslie and Jesse were in at Lark Creek
ELLIE	9. Eldest Aarons daughter
JOYCE	10. Jesse's youngest sister; ____ Ann
THIRTYONE	11. Number of students in the fifth-grade class
SCUBA	12. Topic of Leslie's essay; ____ diving
UHAUL	13. Delivers new people to the old Perkins' place
GEORGIA	14. Mrs. Aarons' homeplace
LARK	15. Local elementary school; ____ Creek
LESLIE	16. Fastest runner in the fifth grade
FIRST	17. What Leslie calls her parents by; ---- names
WRITERS	18. Leslie's parents' jobs
FOREST	19. Sacred place; Pine _____
BARBIE	20. May Belle's beloved Christmas gift

Bridge to Terabithia Matching 1

___ 1. RAIN   A. Number of students in the fifth-grade class
___ 2. ELLIE   B. Eldest Aarons daughter
___ 3. FRIDAYS   C. Magical kingdom in C.S. Lewis stories
___ 4. FREE   D. Entry into secret kingdom; ____ swing
___ 5. TV   E. Miss Edmunds' day at Lark Creek
___ 6. FIRST   F. Miss Edmunds' favorite song; --- to Be You and Me
___ 7. WRITERS   G. Grade Leslie and Jesse were in at Lark Creek
___ 8. DRAWING   H. Jesse's Christmas gift from his dad; ___ car set
___ 9. RACING   I. Christmas gift to Jesse from Leslie; ___ set
___ 10. GUTS   J. Local elementary school; ____ Creek
___ 11. LAIDOFF   K. Burke's have none
___ 12. NARNIA   L. Leslie's parents' jobs
___ 13. BEANS   M. Fastest runner in the fifth grade
___ 14. LESLIE   N. Leslie reigned as this over Terabithia
___ 15. QUEEN   O. Miss Edmunds' instrument
___ 16. LARK   P. Leslie wanted to go to church with Jesse then
___ 17. MAY   Q. Day trip Miss Edmunds and Jesse take; Nat'l. Art ____
___ 18. ROPE   R. Jesse's favorite pastime
___ 19. GUITAR   S. What Leslie calls her parents by; ---- names
___ 20. PAINT   T. Jesse thinks he has none
___ 21. EASTER   U. Refinished room of the Burke's; ____ room
___ 22. GOLDEN   V. Worships Jesse; ___ Belle
___ 23. FIFTH   W. Evil curse
___ 24. GALLERY   X. What happened to Jesse's dad (2 words)
___ 25. THIRTYONE   Y. Jesse needs to pick and can these

Bridge to Terabithia Matching 1 Answer Key

W - 1.	RAIN	A.	Number of students in the fifth-grade class
B - 2.	ELLIE	B.	Eldest Aarons daughter
E - 3.	FRIDAYS	C.	Magical kingdom in C.S. Lewis stories
F - 4.	FREE	D.	Entry into secret kingdom; ____ swing
K - 5.	TV	E.	Miss Edmunds' day at Lark Creek
S - 6.	FIRST	F.	Miss Edmunds'favorite song; --- to Be You and Me
L - 7.	WRITERS	G.	Grade Leslie and Jesse were in at Lark Creek
R - 8.	DRAWING	H.	Jesse's Christmas gift from his dad; ___ car set
H - 9.	RACING	I.	Christmas gift to Jesse from Leslie; ___ set
T - 10.	GUTS	J.	Local elementary school; ____ Creek
X - 11.	LAIDOFF	K.	Burke's have none
C - 12.	NARNIA	L.	Leslie's parents'jobs
Y - 13.	BEANS	M.	Fastest runner in the fifth grade
M - 14.	LESLIE	N.	Leslie reigned as this over Terabithia
N - 15.	QUEEN	O.	Miss Edmunds' instrument
J - 16.	LARK	P.	Leslie wanted to go to church with Jesse then
V - 17.	MAY	Q.	Day trip Miss Edmunds and Jesse take; Nat'l. Art ____
D - 18.	ROPE	R.	Jesse's favorite pastime
O - 19.	GUITAR	S.	What Leslie calls her parents by; ---- names
I - 20.	PAINT	T.	Jesse thinks he has none
P - 21.	EASTER	U.	Refinished room of the Burke's; ____ room
U - 22.	GOLDEN	V.	Worships Jesse; ___ Belle
G - 23.	FIFTH	W.	Evil curse
Q - 24.	GALLERY	X.	What happened to Jesse's dad (2 words)
A - 25.	THIRTYONE	Y.	Jesse needs to pick and can these

Bridge to Terabithia Matching 2

___ 1. GUITAR A. Jesse's dad drives there everyday to work; ____ D.C.
___ 2. ELLIE B. Sacred place; Pine _____
___ 3. FIRST C. Christmas gift to Jesse from Leslie; ___ set
___ 4. MAY D. Evil curse
___ 5. UHAUL E. Fastest runner in the fifth grade
___ 6. NEAT F. What Leslie calls her parents by; ---- names
___ 7. FRIDAYS G. Delivers new people to the old Perkins' place
___ 8. PAINT H. Ellie's purchase in Millsburg; see-through _____
___ 9. DOLLS I. Leslie wanted to go to church with Jesse then
___ 10. LARK J. Guardian of Terabithia; Prince ____
___ 11. GALLERY K. Local elementary school; ____ Creek
___ 12. WASHINGTON L. Topic of Leslie's essay; ____ diving
___ 13. NARNIA M. Bribe May Belle took; paper _____
___ 14. ARLINGTON N. Eighth grade Aarons daughter
___ 15. BLOUSE O. Miss Edmunds' day at Lark Creek
___ 16. TV P. What Leslie's parents were reassessing; ____ structure
___ 17. RAIN Q. Mrs. Aarons' homeplace
___ 18. SCUBA R. Magical kingdom in C.S. Lewis stories
___ 19. VALUE S. Miss Edmunds' instrument
___ 20. BRENDA T. Leslie's old school
___ 21. EASTER U. Worships Jesse; ___ Belle
___ 22. LESLIE V. What Miss Edmunds calls Jesse; ____ Kid
___ 23. TERRIEN W. Day trip Miss Edmunds and Jesse take; Nat'l. Art ____
___ 24. FOREST X. Eldest Aarons daughter
___ 25. GEORGIA Y. Burke's have none

Bridge to Terabithia Matching 2 Answer Key

S - 1. GUITAR	A.	Jesse's dad drives there everyday to work; ____ D.C.
X - 2. ELLIE	B.	Sacred place; Pine _____
F - 3. FIRST	C.	Christmas gift to Jesse from Leslie; ___ set
U - 4. MAY	D.	Evil curse
G - 5. UHAUL	E.	Fastest runner in the fifth grade
V - 6. NEAT	F.	What Leslie calls her parents by; ---- names
O - 7. FRIDAYS	G.	Delivers new people to the old Perkins' place
C - 8. PAINT	H.	Ellie's purchase in Millsburg; see-through _____
M - 9. DOLLS	I.	Leslie wanted to go to church with Jesse then
K - 10. LARK	J.	Guardian of Terabithia; Prince ____
W - 11. GALLERY	K.	Local elementary school; ____ Creek
A - 12. WASHINGTON	L.	Topic of Leslie's essay; ____ diving
R - 13. NARNIA	M.	Bribe May Belle took; paper ____
T - 14. ARLINGTON	N.	Eighth grade Aarons daughter
H - 15. BLOUSE	O.	Miss Edmunds' day at Lark Creek
Y - 16. TV	P.	What Leslie's parents were reassessing; ____ structure
D - 17. RAIN	Q.	Mrs. Aarons' homeplace
L - 18. SCUBA	R.	Magical kingdom in C.S. Lewis stories
P - 19. VALUE	S.	Miss Edmunds' instrument
N - 20. BRENDA	T.	Leslie's old school
I - 21. EASTER	U.	Worships Jesse; ___ Belle
E - 22. LESLIE	V.	What Miss Edmunds calls Jesse; ____ Kid
J - 23. TERRIEN	W.	Day trip Miss Edmunds and Jesse take; Nat'l. Art ____
B - 24. FOREST	X.	Eldest Aarons daughter
Q - 25. GEORGIA	Y.	Burke's have none

Bridge to Terabithia Matching 3

___ 1. FREE   A. Leslie's old school
___ 2. BEANS   B. Miss Edmunds' favorite song; --- to Be You and Me
___ 3. PENNSYLVANIA   C. Entry into secret kingdom; ____ swing
___ 4. BRENDA   D. How Leslie died
___ 5. DROWNED   E. Burke's have none
___ 6. MAY   F. Miss Edmunds' day at Lark Creek
___ 7. TV   G. Eighth grade Aarons daughter
___ 8. WASHINGTON   H. Leslie wanted to go to church with Jesse then
___ 9. LESLIE   I. Number of students in the fifth-grade class
___10. VALUE   J. Guardian of Terabithia; Prince ____
___11. EDMUNDS   K. What Leslie's parents were reassessing; ____ structure
___12. PAINT   L. Worships Jesse; ___ Belle
___13. JANICE   M. Jesse's youngest sister; ____ Ann
___14. TERRIEN   N. Peace-loving music teacher; Miss _____
___15. GOLDEN   O. Leslie's parents' jobs
___16. FRIDAYS   P. Refinished room of the Burke's; ____ room
___17. WRITERS   Q. Jesse's dad drives there everyday to work; ____ D.C.
___18. FIRST   R. Jesse thinks he has none
___19. ARLINGTON   S. Where Leslie's ashes were taken
___20. FIFTH   T. Seventh grade bully; ____ Avery
___21. ROPE   U. What Leslie calls her parents by; ---- names
___22. GUTS   V. Fastest runner in the fifth grade
___23. EASTER   W. Christmas gift to Jesse from Leslie; ___ set
___24. THIRTYONE   X. Jesse needs to pick and can these
___25. JOYCE   Y. Grade Leslie and Jesse were in at Lark Creek

Bridge to Terabithia Matching 3 Answer Key

B - 1. FREE	A.	Leslie's old school
X - 2. BEANS	B.	Miss Edmunds' favorite song; --- to Be You and Me
S - 3. PENNSYLVANIA	C.	Entry into secret kingdom; ____ swing
G - 4. BRENDA	D.	How Leslie died
D - 5. DROWNED	E.	Burke's have none
L - 6. MAY	F.	Miss Edmunds' day at Lark Creek
E - 7. TV	G.	Eighth grade Aarons daughter
Q - 8. WASHINGTON	H.	Leslie wanted to go to church with Jesse then
V - 9. LESLIE	I.	Number of students in the fifth-grade class
K - 10. VALUE	J.	Guardian of Terabithia; Prince ____
N - 11. EDMUNDS	K.	What Leslie's parents were reassessing; ____ structure
W - 12. PAINT	L.	Worships Jesse; ___ Belle
T - 13. JANICE	M.	Jesse's youngest sister; ____ Ann
J - 14. TERRIEN	N.	Peace-loving music teacher; Miss _____
P - 15. GOLDEN	O.	Leslie's parents' jobs
F - 16. FRIDAYS	P.	Refinished room of the Burke's; ____ room
O - 17. WRITERS	Q.	Jesse's dad drives there everyday to work; ____ D.C.
U - 18. FIRST	R.	Jesse thinks he has none
A - 19. ARLINGTON	S.	Where Leslie's ashes were taken
Y - 20. FIFTH	T.	Seventh grade bully; ____ Avery
C - 21. ROPE	U.	What Leslie calls her parents by; ---- names
R - 22. GUTS	V.	Fastest runner in the fifth grade
H - 23. EASTER	W.	Christmas gift to Jesse from Leslie; ___ set
I - 24. THIRTYONE	X.	Jesse needs to pick and can these
M - 25. JOYCE	Y.	Grade Leslie and Jesse were in at Lark Creek

Bridge to Terabithia Matching 4

___ 1. LAIDOFF   A. Christmas gift to Jesse from Leslie; ___ set
___ 2. PATERSON   B. Entry into secret kingdom; ____ swing
___ 3. FIFTH   C. Fifth grade teacher; ____ Mouth Myers
___ 4. LUMBER   D. Where Leslie's ashes were taken
___ 5. MONSTER   E. What happened to Jesse's dad (2 words)
___ 6. PENNSYLVANIA   F. Leslie reigned as this over Terabithia
___ 7. LESLIE   G. Author
___ 8. ARLINGTON   H. Leslie's old school
___ 9. PAINT   I. What Leslie's parents were reassessing; ____ structure
___ 10. JESSE   J. Fastest runner in the fifth grade
___ 11. FIRST   K. Secret place
___ 12. DOLLS   L. Leslie wanted to go to church with Jesse then
___ 13. QUEEN   M. Ten-year-old boy in family of all girls
___ 14. ROPE   N. Jesse's youngest sister; ____ Ann
___ 15. RACING   O. Guardian of Terabithia; Prince ____
___ 16. JOYCE   P. May Belle's beloved Christmas gift
___ 17. NARNIA   Q. Jesse's Christmas gift from his dad; ___ car set
___ 18. DRAWING   R. Local elementary school; ____ Creek
___ 19. TERABITHIA   S. What Leslie calls her parents by; ---- names
___ 20. TERRIEN   T. Jesse's favorite pastime
___ 21. BARBIE   U. Number of students in the fifth-grade class
___ 22. VALUE   V. Used to build bridge over creek bed
___ 23. EASTER   W. Grade Leslie and Jesse were in at Lark Creek
___ 24. LARK   X. Magical kingdom in C.S. Lewis stories
___ 25. THIRTYONE   Y. Bribe May Belle took; paper _____

Bridge to Terabithia Matching 4 Answer Key

E - 1. LAIDOFF	A.	Christmas gift to Jesse from Leslie; ___ set
G - 2. PATERSON	B.	Entry into secret kingdom; ___ swing
W - 3. FIFTH	C.	Fifth grade teacher; ___ Mouth Myers
V - 4. LUMBER	D.	Where Leslie's ashes were taken
C - 5. MONSTER	E.	What happened to Jesse's dad (2 words)
D - 6. PENNSYLVANIA	F.	Leslie reigned as this over Terabithia
J - 7. LESLIE	G.	Author
H - 8. ARLINGTON	H.	Leslie's old school
A - 9. PAINT	I.	What Leslie's parents were reassessing; ___ structure
M - 10. JESSE	J.	Fastest runner in the fifth grade
S - 11. FIRST	K.	Secret place
Y - 12. DOLLS	L.	Leslie wanted to go to church with Jesse then
F - 13. QUEEN	M.	Ten-year-old boy in family of all girls
B - 14. ROPE	N.	Jesse's youngest sister; ___ Ann
Q - 15. RACING	O.	Guardian of Terabithia; Prince ___
N - 16. JOYCE	P.	May Belle's beloved Christmas gift
X - 17. NARNIA	Q.	Jesse's Christmas gift from his dad; ___ car set
T - 18. DRAWING	R.	Local elementary school; ___ Creek
K - 19. TERABITHIA	S.	What Leslie calls her parents by; ---- names
O - 20. TERRIEN	T.	Jesse's favorite pastime
P - 21. BARBIE	U.	Number of students in the fifth-grade class
I - 22. VALUE	V.	Used to build bridge over creek bed
L - 23. EASTER	W.	Grade Leslie and Jesse were in at Lark Creek
R - 24. LARK	X.	Magical kingdom in C.S. Lewis stories
U - 25. THIRTYONE	Y.	Bribe May Belle took; paper ___

Bridge to Terabithia Magic Squares 1

Match the definition with the vocabulary word. Put your answers in the magic squares below. When your answers are correct, all columns and rows will add to the same number.

A. QUEEN
B. WASHINGTON
C. SCUBA
D. BESSIE
E. LUMBER
F. KING
G. VALUE
H. BLOUSE
I. RACING
J. LARK
K. EASTER
L. GUITAR
M. PATERSON
N. LESLIE
O. FRIDAYS
P. BARBIE

1. Author
2. Jesse reigned as this over their kingdom
3. Ellie's purchase in Millsburg; see-through _____
4. Miss Edmunds' day at Lark Creek
5. Miss Edmunds' instrument
6. Topic of Leslie's essay; ____ diving
7. Leslie reigned as this over Terabithia
8. Local elementary school; ____ Creek
9. Leslie wanted to go to church with Jesse then
10. Jesse milks her daily; Miss ____
11. Jesse's dad drives there everyday to work; ____ D.C.
12. Jesse's Christmas gift from his dad; ____ car set
13. Fastest runner in the fifth grade
14. Used to build bridge over creek bed
15. What Leslie's parents were reassessing; ____ structure
16. May Belle's beloved Christmas gift

A=	B=	C=	D=
E=	F=	G=	H=
I=	J=	K=	L=
M=	N=	O=	P=

Bridge to Terabithia Magic Squares 1 Answer Key

Match the definition with the vocabulary word. Put your answers in the magic squares below. When your answers are correct, all columns and rows will add to the same number.

A. QUEEN   E. LUMBER   I. RACING   M. PATERSON
B. WASHINGTON   F. KING   J. LARK   N. LESLIE
C. SCUBA   G. VALUE   K. EASTER   O. FRIDAYS
D. BESSIE   H. BLOUSE   L. GUITAR   P. BARBIE

1. Author
2. Jesse reigned as this over their kingdom
3. Ellie's purchase in Millsburg; see-through _____
4. Miss Edmunds' day at Lark Creek
5. Miss Edmunds' instrument
6. Topic of Leslie's essay; ____ diving
7. Leslie reigned as this over Terabithia
8. Local elementary school; ____ Creek
9. Leslie wanted to go to church with Jesse then
10. Jesse milks her daily; Miss ____
11. Jesse's dad drives there everyday to work; ____ D.C.
12. Jesse's Christmas gift from his dad; ____ car set
13. Fastest runner in the fifth grade
14. Used to build bridge over creek bed
15. What Leslie's parents were reassessing; ____ structure
16. May Belle's beloved Christmas gift

A=7	B=11	C=6	D=10
E=14	F=2	G=15	H=3
I=12	J=8	K=9	L=5
M=1	N=13	O=4	P=16

Bridge to Terabithia Magic Squares 2

Match the definition with the vocabulary word. Put your answers in the magic squares below. When your answers are correct, all columns and rows will add to the same number.

A. DROWNED   E. JESSE   I. FOREST   M. FREE
B. PAINT   F. WRITERS   J. LAIDOFF   N. ELLIE
C. JOYCE   G. KING   K. WASHINGTON   O. TV
D. MAY   H. GUTS   L. RAIN   P. FRIDAYS

1. How Leslie died
2. Eldest Aarons daughter
3. What happened to Jesse's dad (2 words)
4. Ten-year-old boy in family of all girls
5. Jesse reigned as this over their kingdom
6. Evil curse
7. Miss Edmunds' day at Lark Creek
8. Jesse's youngest sister; _____ Ann
9. Burke's have none
10. Worships Jesse; ___ Belle
11. Jesse thinks he has none
12. Jesse's dad drives there everyday to work; ____ D.C.
13. Sacred place; Pine _____
14. Leslie's parents' jobs
15. Christmas gift to Jesse from Leslie; ___ set
16. Miss Edmunds' favorite song; --- to Be You and Me

A=	B=	C=	D=
E=	F=	G=	H=
I=	J=	K=	L=
M=	N=	O=	P=

Bridge to Terabithia Magic Squares 2 Answer Key

Match the definition with the vocabulary word. Put your answers in the magic squares below. When your answers are correct, all columns and rows will add to the same number.

A. DROWNED
B. PAINT
C. JOYCE
D. MAY
E. JESSE
F. WRITERS
G. KING
H. GUTS
I. FOREST
J. LAIDOFF
K. WASHINGTON
L. RAIN
M. FREE
N. ELLIE
O. TV
P. FRIDAYS

1. How Leslie died
2. Eldest Aarons daughter
3. What happened to Jesse's dad (2 words)
4. Ten-year-old boy in family of all girls
5. Jesse reigned as this over their kingdom
6. Evil curse
7. Miss Edmunds' day at Lark Creek
8. Jesse's youngest sister; ____ Ann
9. Burke's have none
10. Worships Jesse; ___ Belle
11. Jesse thinks he has none
12. Jesse's dad drives there everyday to work; ____ D.C.
13. Sacred place; Pine _____
14. Leslie's parents' jobs
15. Christmas gift to Jesse from Leslie; ___ set
16. Miss Edmunds' favorite song; --- to Be You and Me

A=1	B=15	C=8	D=10
E=4	F=14	G=5	H=11
I=13	J=3	K=12	L=6
M=16	N=2	O=9	P=7

Bridge to Terabithia Magic Squares 3

Match the definition with the vocabulary word. Put your answers in the magic squares below. When your answers are correct, all columns and rows will add to the same number.

A. QUEEN   E. LESLIE   I. FIRST   M. BESSIE
B. FRIDAYS   F. TERRIEN   J. WRITERS   N. FREE
C. SCUBA   G. ARLINGTON   K. NARNIA   O. GOLDEN
D. BEANS   H. PATERSON   L. GUITAR   P. GALLERY

1. Miss Edmunds' day at Lark Creek
2. Leslie's old school
3. Magical kingdom in C.S. Lewis stories
4. Miss Edmunds' favorite song; --- to Be You and Me
5. Jesse milks her daily; Miss ____
6. Miss Edmunds' instrument
7. Author
8. Leslie reigned as this over Terabithia
9. Day trip Miss Edmunds and Jesse take; Nat'l. Art ____
10. What Leslie calls her parents by; ---- names
11. Fastest runner in the fifth grade
12. Jesse needs to pick and can these
13. Topic of Leslie's essay; ____ diving
14. Guardian of Terabithia; Prince ____
15. Leslie's parents' jobs
16. Refinished room of the Burke's; ____ room

A=	B=	C=	D=
E=	F=	G=	H=
I=	J=	K=	L=
M=	N=	O=	P=

Bridge to Terabithia Magic Squares 3 Answer Key

Match the definition with the vocabulary word. Put your answers in the magic squares below. When your answers are correct, all columns and rows will add to the same number.

A. QUEEN   E. LESLIE   I. FIRST   M. BESSIE
B. FRIDAYS F. TERRIEN   J. WRITERS   N. FREE
C. SCUBA   G. ARLINGTON K. NARNIA   O. GOLDEN
D. BEANS   H. PATERSON   L. GUITAR   P. GALLERY

1. Miss Edmunds' day at Lark Creek
2. Leslie's old school
3. Magical kingdom in C.S. Lewis stories
4. Miss Edmunds' favorite song; --- to Be You and Me
5. Jesse milks her daily; Miss ____
6. Miss Edmunds' instrument
7. Author
8. Leslie reigned as this over Terabithia
9. Day trip Miss Edmunds and Jesse take; Nat'l. Art ____
10. What Leslie calls her parents by; ---- names
11. Fastest runner in the fifth grade
12. Jesse needs to pick and can these
13. Topic of Leslie's essay; ____ diving
14. Guardian of Terabithia; Prince ____
15. Leslie's parents' jobs
16. Refinished room of the Burke's; ____ room

A=8	B=1	C=13	D=12
E=11	F=14	G=2	H=7
I=10	J=15	K=3	L=6
M=5	N=4	O=16	P=9

Bridge to Terabithia Magic Squares 4

Match the definition with the vocabulary word. Put your answers in the magic squares below. When your answers are correct, all columns and rows will add to the same number.

A. TERABITHIA E. BESSIE   I. FIFTH   M. FIRST
B. QUEEN   F. NEAT   J. RACING   N. KING
C. FREE   G. JESSE   K. GEORGIA   O. NARNIA
D. THIRTYONE   H. GOLDEN   L. ARLINGTON P. TV

1. What Miss Edmunds calls Jesse; ____ Kid
2. Grade Leslie and Jesse were in at Lark Creek
3. Magical kingdom in C.S. Lewis stories
4. Number of students in the fifth-grade class
5. What Leslie calls her parents by; ---- names
6. Leslie reigned as this over Terabithia
7. Refinished room of the Burke's; ____ room
8. Mrs. Aarons' homeplace
9. Miss Edmunds' favorite song; --- to Be You and Me
10. Burke's have none
11. Jesse's Christmas gift from his dad; ___ car set
12. Jesse milks her daily; Miss ____
13. Leslie's old school
14. Ten-year-old boy in family of all girls
15. Secret place
16. Jesse reigned as this over their kingdom

A=	B=	C=	D=
E=	F=	G=	H=
I=	J=	K=	L=
M=	N=	O=	P=

Bridge to Terabithia Magic Squares 4 Answer Key

Match the definition with the vocabulary word. Put your answers in the magic squares below. When your answers are correct, all columns and rows will add to the same number.

A. TERABITHIA	E. BESSIE	I. FIFTH	M. FIRST
B. QUEEN	F. NEAT	J. RACING	N. KING
C. FREE	G. JESSE	K. GEORGIA	O. NARNIA
D. THIRTYONE	H. GOLDEN	L. ARLINGTON	P. TV

1. What Miss Edmunds calls Jesse; ____ Kid
2. Grade Leslie and Jesse were in at Lark Creek
3. Magical kingdom in C.S. Lewis stories
4. Number of students in the fifth-grade class
5. What Leslie calls her parents by; ---- names
6. Leslie reigned as this over Terabithia
7. Refinished room of the Burke's; ____ room
8. Mrs. Aarons' homeplace
9. Miss Edmunds' favorite song; --- to Be You and Me
10. Burke's have none
11. Jesse's Christmas gift from his dad; ___ car set
12. Jesse milks her daily; Miss ____
13. Leslie's old school
14. Ten-year-old boy in family of all girls
15. Secret place
16. Jesse reigned as this over their kingdom

A=15	B=6	C=9	D=4
E=12	F=1	G=14	H=7
I=2	J=11	K=8	L=13
M=5	N=16	O=3	P=10

Bridge to Terabithia Word Search 1

```
D F K Q J G W D P Y K D L F S C U B A N
O R R M U O O R M W I S E E I P A D T N
L L A E B E Y L I K N G S J L R B Y E R
L E L W E X E C D T G S L G B E S V R L
S R A C I N G N E E E K I I A X A T A G
D C J S V N R F Q J N R E N B M I J B L
H W U R T J G O Q S G J S G W M N A I N
C F D E X E S R P J F H P X A C A N T G
Q X Y B G D R E L I M G A N W L V I H P
Z F G M N P T S F F O D I A L T L C I C
V A L U E P A T E R S O N C N R Y E A Y
N D M L T K H P H Z Y I T A Y A S G R R
Q D U H Z S C V F A A G R P M B N E E Y
E N H W L Z V P D R D N B B R E N O L S
C R A T I U G N N E I R R E T S E R L N
E S U O L B E E C A R O K B J S P G I X
Y S L Q M R A N W Q F P M Z J I H I E Z
M T S K B T M O N S T E R N V E D A K F
```

Author (8)
Bribe May Belle took; paper _____ (5)
Burke's have none (2)
Christmas gift to Jesse from Leslie; ___ set (5)
Day trip Miss Edmunds and Jesse take; Nat'l. Art ____ (7)
Delivers new people to the old Perkins' place (5)
Eighth grade Aarons daughter (6)
Eldest Aarons daughter (5)
Ellie's purchase in Millsburg; see-through _____ (6)
Entry into secret kingdom; ____ swing (4)
Evil curse (4)
Fastest runner in the fifth grade (6)
Fifth grade teacher; ____ Mouth Myers (7)
Grade Leslie and Jesse were in at Lark Creek (5)
Guardian of Terabithia; Prince ____ (7)
Jesse milks her daily; Miss ____ (6)
Jesse needs to pick and can these (5)
Jesse reigned as this over their kingdom (4)
Jesse thinks he has none (4)
Jesse's Christmas gift from his dad; ___ car set (6)
Jesse's favorite pastime (7)
Jesse's youngest sister; ____ Ann (5)
Leslie reigned as this over Terabithia (5)
Leslie wanted to go to church with Jesse then (6)
Leslie's parents'jobs (7)
Leslie's parents; ____ and Bill (4)
Local elementary school; ____ Creek (4)
Magical kingdom in C.S. Lewis stories (6)
May Belle's beloved Christmas gift (6)
Miss Edmunds' day at Lark Creek (7)
Miss Edmunds' instrument (6)
Miss Edmunds' favorite song; --- to Be You and Me (4)
Mrs. Aarons' homeplace (7)
Peace-loving music teacher; Miss _____ (7)
Refinished room of the Burke's; ____ room (6)
Sacred place; Pine _____ (6)
Secret place (10)
Seventh grade bully; ____ Avery (6)
Ten-year-old boy in family of all girls (5)
Topic of Leslie's essay; ____ diving (5)
Used to build bridge over creek bed (6)
What Leslie calls her parents by; ---- names (5)
What Leslie's parents were reassessing; ____ structure (5)
What Miss Edmunds calls Jesse; ____ Kid (4)
What happened to Jesse's dad (2 words) (7)
Where Leslie's ashes were taken (12)
Worships Jesse; ___ Belle (3)

Bridge to Terabithia Word Search 1

Author (8)
Bribe May Belle took; paper _____ (5)
Burke's have none (2)
Christmas gift to Jesse from Leslie; ___ set (5)
Day trip Miss Edmunds and Jesse take; Nat'l. Art _____ (7)
Delivers new people to the old Perkins' place (5)
Eighth grade Aarons daughter (6)
Eldest Aarons daughter (5)
Ellie's purchase in Millsburg; see-through _____ (6)
Entry into secret kingdom; ____ swing (4)
Evil curse (4)
Fastest runner in the fifth grade (6)
Fifth grade teacher; ____ Mouth Myers (7)
Grade Leslie and Jesse were in at Lark Creek (5)
Guardian of Terabithia; Prince ____ (7)
Jesse milks her daily; Miss _____ (6)
Jesse needs to pick and can these (5)
Jesse reigned as this over their kingdom (4)
Jesse thinks he has none (4)
Jesse's Christmas gift from his dad; ___ car set (6)
Jesse's favorite pastime (7)
Jesse's youngest sister; _____ Ann (5)
Leslie reigned as this over Terabithia (5)
Leslie wanted to go to church with Jesse then (6)
Leslie's parents'jobs (7)
Leslie's parents; ____ and Bill (4)
Local elementary school; ____ Creek (4)
Magical kingdom in C.S. Lewis stories (6)
May Belle's beloved Christmas gift (6)
Miss Edmunds' day at Lark Creek (7)
Miss Edmunds' instrument (6)
Miss Edmunds'favorite song; --- to Be You and Me (4)
Mrs. Aarons' homeplace (7)
Peace-loving music teacher; Miss _____ (7)
Refinished room of the Burke's; ____ room (6)
Sacred place; Pine _____ (6)
Secret place (10)
Seventh grade bully; _____ Avery (6)
Ten-year-old boy in family of all girls (5)
Topic of Leslie's essay; _____ diving (5)
Used to build bridge over creek bed (6)
What Leslie calls her parents by; ---- names (5)
What Leslie's parents were reassessing; ____ structure (5)
What Miss Edmunds calls Jesse; ____ Kid (4)
What happened to Jesse's dad (2 words) (7)
Where Leslie's ashes were taken (12)
Worships Jesse; ___ Belle (3)

Bridge to Terabithia Word Search 2

```
N O S R E T A P D W R I T E R S N N T S
H A Q S N G A T R L Y N J K G N I D H W
Q I R C T I N N A V E G X F X A D S I P
S H J N N M E K W J R S E J R G L N R W
F T Z T I E I J I H J D L O A K G F T K
W I Z N U A R T N F O G Y I R N S P Y X
L B F Q G J R N G F Y H F Q E G I Q O J
J A B T G U E J V J C P R V R B I C N V
W R N A H O T A D N E R B R E T S A E Y
K E Z K R A L S Z S E B M A B Z L S H Y
W T I K E B P D S G D B N N M D U H Z W
K N F N L L I E E J M S Q S U O O Q G L
G U I T A R J E H N U E I L L E U L A V
N F R L I C Q I N H N D P B U S Y R L N
I R S B D M K S N N D P Y M A C K H L S
C E T J O A S S B S S K H F H U J G E W
A E T X F Y F E F O R E S T U B V S R R
R O P E F H K B T V L F R I D A Y S Y F
```

Author (8)
Bribe May Belle took; paper _____ (5)
Burke's have none (2)
Christmas gift to Jesse from Leslie; ___ set (5)
Day trip Miss Edmunds and Jesse take; Nat'l. Art _____ (7)
Delivers new people to the old Perkins' place (5)
Eighth grade Aarons daughter (6)
Eldest Aarons daughter (5)
Ellie's purchase in Millsburg; see-through _____ (6)
Entry into secret kingdom; ____ swing (4)
Evil curse (4)
Fastest runner in the fifth grade (6)
Grade Leslie and Jesse were in at Lark Creek (5)
Guardian of Terabithia; Prince ____ (7)
Jesse milks her daily; Miss ____ (6)
Jesse needs to pick and can these (5)
Jesse reigned as this over their kingdom (4)
Jesse thinks he has none (4)
Jesse's Christmas gift from his dad; ___ car set (6)
Jesse's favorite pastime (7)
Jesse's youngest sister; ____ Ann (5)
Leslie reigned as this over Terabithia (5)
Leslie wanted to go to church with Jesse then (6)
Leslie's parents' jobs (7)
Leslie's parents; ____ and Bill (4)
Local elementary school; ____ Creek (4)
Magical kingdom in C.S. Lewis stories (6)
May Belle's beloved Christmas gift (6)
Miss Edmunds' day at Lark Creek (7)
Miss Edmunds' instrument (6)
Miss Edmunds' favorite song; --- to Be You and Me (4)
Mrs. Aarons' homeplace (7)
Number of students in the fifth-grade class (9)
Peace-loving music teacher; Miss _____ (7)
Refinished room of the Burke's; ____ room (6)
Sacred place; Pine _____ (6)
Secret place (10)
Seventh grade bully; ____ Avery (6)
Ten-year-old boy in family of all girls (5)
Topic of Leslie's essay; ____ diving (5)
Used to build bridge over creek bed (6)
What Leslie calls her parents by; ---- names (5)
What Leslie's parents were reassessing; ____ structure (5)
What Miss Edmunds calls Jesse; ____ Kid (4)
What happened to Jesse's dad (2 words) (7)
Worships Jesse; ___ Belle (3)

Bridge to Terabithia Word Search 2 Answer Key

```
N O S R E T A P  D   W R I T E R S       N T
  A              A   R L               I   H
  I R   I N N A  E G                 A     I
  H N N   E   W  S E J           R         R
F T   T I E   I  J   L O A                 T
      U A R   N  O   I R N                 Y
  B F Q G R   G  Y   E G I             C   O
  A B T G U E    C   R B               A   N
  R A H O T A D N E R B R E T S        A   E
  E K R A L S S E     A B              S
  T I E B D S D   N   M D U
  N F N L I E J M S   U O O         G L
G U I T A R J E   N U E I L L E U L A V
  N F R   I       N D   B U S   R L
  I R S D M S     D Y   A C K   L S
  C E T O A S     S     H U     E
  A E   F Y E F O R E S T U B   R
  R O P E F B T V   F R I D A Y S Y
```

Author (8)
Bribe May Belle took; paper _____ (5)
Burke's have none (2)
Christmas gift to Jesse from Leslie; ___ set (5)
Day trip Miss Edmunds and Jesse take; Nat'l. Art ____ (7)
Delivers new people to the old Perkins' place (5)
Eighth grade Aarons daughter (6)
Eldest Aarons daughter (5)
Ellie's purchase in Millsburg; see-through _____ (6)
Entry into secret kingdom; ____ swing (4)
Evil curse (4)
Fastest runner in the fifth grade (6)
Grade Leslie and Jesse were in at Lark Creek (5)
Guardian of Terabithia; Prince ____ (7)
Jesse milks her daily; Miss ____ (6)
Jesse needs to pick and can these (5)
Jesse reigned as this over their kingdom (4)
Jesse thinks he has none (4)
Jesse's Christmas gift from his dad; ___ car set (6)
Jesse's favorite pastime (7)
Jesse's youngest sister; ____ Ann (5)
Leslie reigned as this over Terabithia (5)
Leslie wanted to go to church with Jesse then (6)
Leslie's parents' jobs (7)
Leslie's parents; ____ and Bill (4)
Local elementary school; ____ Creek (4)
Magical kingdom in C.S. Lewis stories (6)
May Belle's beloved Christmas gift (6)
Miss Edmunds' day at Lark Creek (7)
Miss Edmunds' instrument (6)
Miss Edmunds' favorite song; --- to Be You and Me (4)
Mrs. Aarons' homeplace (7)
Number of students in the fifth-grade class (9)
Peace-loving music teacher; Miss ____ (7)
Refinished room of the Burke's; ____ room (6)
Sacred place; Pine _____ (6)
Secret place (10)
Seventh grade bully; ____ Avery (6)
Ten-year-old boy in family of all girls (5)
Topic of Leslie's essay; ____ diving (5)
Used to build bridge over creek bed (6)
What Leslie calls her parents by; ---- names (5)
What Leslie's parents were reassessing; ____ structure (5)
What Miss Edmunds calls Jesse; ____ Kid (4)
What happened to Jesse's dad (2 words) (7)
Worships Jesse; ___ Belle (3)

Bridge to Terabithia Word Search 3

```
F T E R R I E N C H Y K P E C Y O J Y L T C
R K L P K F G D U R N I T D B Q P M P A H R
I K A Q P T B E E H N N W M V U E A X R I V
D Y I F Q E D L O H A G Y U D E N Y M K R F
A H D Y F R L Z O R W U S N L E N M F Y T P
Y P O V S A M V V U G B L D Q N S P J R Y P
S Q F G G B L D M D S I Y S G A Y R Q K O C
V V F V M I W D V O F E A L W R L R C M N W
T M M R N T P H Q P N M G S T L V Y R R E D
N Y N Y M H G B F N G S Q P L I A B F L F G
H N B G Z I U G B S Z O T M B N N S Q U L J
P P A C K A I Z B G G Z L E K G I C R M R M
A X F R F T T V W T U W A D R T A U S B O J
T Y N Y N O A D W A T N C G E O G B V E P P
E X Q V F I R S T E S M P A I N T A R R E M
R H T M Z A A E I N R H Y N I B L J E A D B
S N D M W M P L S R E C I C J U A T E A I F
O R G I X T L S X T T D A N E A S R D S Q N
N M N E B E S S I E I R O J G A N N B R S Y
G G E D R O W N E D R Q L L E T E I C I D E
P R Y R L L Y C N W W F P D L R O Q C U E W
F L E S L I E F I F T H N D B S Y N J E K X
```

ARLINGTON	ELLIE	JANICE	NARNIA	TERRIEN
BARBIE	FIFTH	JESSE	NEAT	THIRTYONE
BEANS	FIRST	JOYCE	PAINT	TV
BESSIE	FOREST	JUDY	PATERSON	UHAUL
BLOUSE	FREE	KING	PENNSYLVANIA	VALUE
BRENDA	FRIDAYS	LAIDOFF	QUEEN	WASHINGTON
DOLLS	GALLERY	LARK	RACING	WRITERS
DRAWING	GEORGIA	LESLIE	RAIN	
DROWNED	GOLDEN	LUMBER	ROPE	
EASTER	GUITAR	MAY	SCUBA	
EDMUNDS	GUTS	MONSTER	TERABITHIA	

Bridge to Terabithia Word Search 3 Answer Key

[Word search grid puzzle]

ARLINGTON	ELLIE	JANICE	NARNIA	TERRIEN
BARBIE	FIFTH	JESSE	NEAT	THIRTYONE
BEANS	FIRST	JOYCE	PAINT	TV
BESSIE	FOREST	JUDY	PATERSON	UHAUL
BLOUSE	FREE	KING	PENNSYLVANIA	VALUE
BRENDA	FRIDAYS	LAIDOFF	QUEEN	WASHINGTON
DOLLS	GALLERY	LARK	RACING	WRITERS
DRAWING	GEORGIA	LESLIE	RAIN	
DROWNED	GOLDEN	LUMBER	ROPE	
EASTER	GUITAR	MAY	SCUBA	
EDMUNDS	GUTS	MONSTER	TERABITHIA	

Bridge to Terabithia Word Search 4

```
Q H Y P F F J N Y W H K T P Q L M L T X Q P J B
Z N J T X X V K V B W F E F L D J Y J M V M C N
T H Y Y D G K C W L V L R Z Y K J M X B L X P C
C M E Y Z C Q N H V P K A H C G P X S K N G E W
T L G D W C C D G F Q B B T F D G B W G H Z N L
H N Q C M K Q D D W B X I D G Z R V B N A F N R
I C W J L U C V O Z Y R T X T E P X L I P I S H
R Y L J S T N K L S E L H G N V N L N C K R Y C
T F R J H L Z D L T F B I D N L I R A A Q S L W
Y I W R I T E R S T N I A P S Y A D I R F T V P
O F X B G C D N G E Y B M R R N R I L S K J A Y
N T Y B I U O F D A U D G E B F B K D U N G N J
E H L N E M T L M C R E L E J I R E P O M E I V
C F A I V S O S S A S L A E O U E E A N F B A P
T J L K R G S N W U A S I U S R D M E N T F E T
T L D R O P E I O G T E X N H L G Y Z G S V S R
E V H R L Y N L E E C E X O G A I I W U E A S D
H Y W G O G B J R Y K L R S R T U E A I R L E M
P P V P P W V C O H I N D R Z J O L B T O U J G
Z P Q U E E N J V X N Y H E I P D N B A F E C P
K V Y X D W S E P Z G F J T F E Q T L R K W X W
Z G G M X H M J D Q K N Z A Q V N F Y L T P H H
W A S H I N G T O N Z R J P C Z L X B L K V L P
R R T N R J D H G C Q W Y C N K B Q F B P N S J
```

ARLINGTON	ELLIE	JANICE	NARNIA	TERRIEN
BARBIE	FIFTH	JESSE	NEAT	THIRTYONE
BEANS	FIRST	JOYCE	PAINT	TV
BESSIE	FOREST	JUDY	PATERSON	UHAUL
BLOUSE	FREE	KING	PENNSYLVANIA	VALUE
BRENDA	FRIDAYS	LAIDOFF	QUEEN	WASHINGTON
DOLLS	GALLERY	LARK	RACING	WRITERS
DRAWING	GEORGIA	LESLIE	RAIN	
DROWNED	GOLDEN	LUMBER	ROPE	
EASTER	GUITAR	MAY	SCUBA	
EDMUNDS	GUTS	MONSTER	TERABITHIA	

Bridge to Terabithia Word Search 4 Answer Key

ARLINGTON	ELLIE	JANICE	NARNIA	TERRIEN
BARBIE	FIFTH	JESSE	NEAT	THIRTYONE
BEANS	FIRST	JOYCE	PAINT	TV
BESSIE	FOREST	JUDY	PATERSON	UHAUL
BLOUSE	FREE	KING	PENNSYLVANIA	VALUE
BRENDA	FRIDAYS	LAIDOFF	QUEEN	WASHINGTON
DOLLS	GALLERY	LARK	RACING	WRITERS
DRAWING	GEORGIA	LESLIE	RAIN	
DROWNED	GOLDEN	LUMBER	ROPE	
EASTER	GUITAR	MAY	SCUBA	
EDMUNDS	GUTS	MONSTER	TERABITHIA	

Bridge to Terabithia Crossword 1

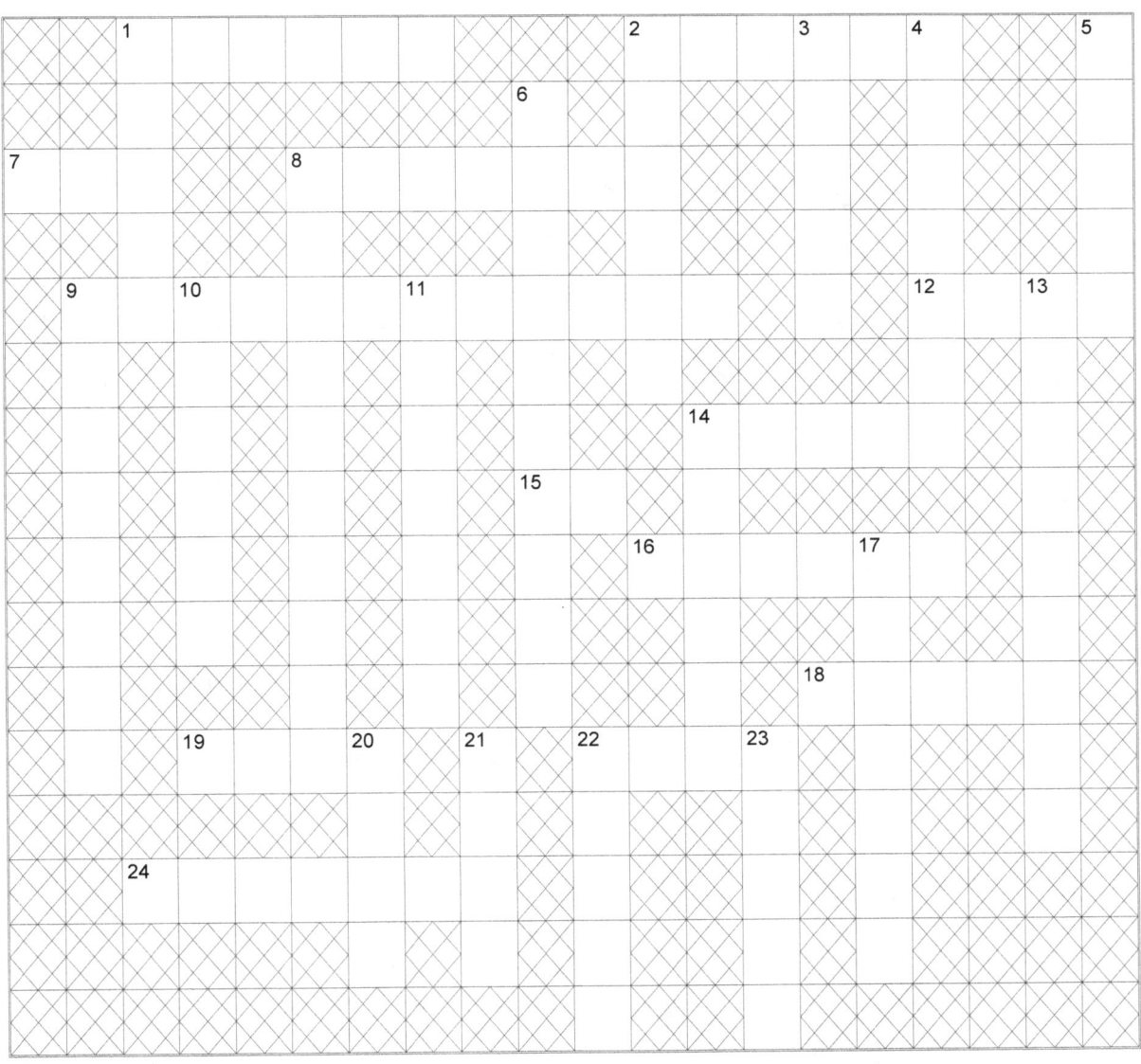

Across
1. Seventh grade bully; ____ Avery
2. Ellie's purchase in Millsburg; see-through _____
7. Worships Jesse; ___ Belle
8. Leslie's parents' jobs
9. Where Leslie's ashes were taken
12. What Miss Edmunds calls Jesse; ____ Kid
14. Jesse needs to pick and can these
15. Burke's have none
16. Eighth grade Aarons daughter
18. Christmas gift to Jesse from Leslie; ___ set
19. Jesse reigned as this over their kingdom
22. Miss Edmunds' favorite song; --- to Be You and Me
24. Fifth grade teacher; ____ Mouth Myers

Down
1. Jesse's youngest sister; ____ Ann
2. Jesse milks her daily; Miss ____
3. Delivers new people to the old Perkins' place
4. Peace-loving music teacher; Miss _____
5. What Leslie calls her parents by; ---- names
6. Secret place
8. Jesse's dad drives there everyday to work; ____ D.C.
9. Author
10. Magical kingdom in C.S. Lewis stories
11. What happened to Jesse's dad (2 words)
13. Leslie's old school
14. May Belle's beloved Christmas gift
17. Jesse's favorite pastime
20. Jesse thinks he has none
21. Local elementary school; ____ Creek
22. Grade Leslie and Jesse were in at Lark Creek
23. Eldest Aarons daughter

Bridge to Terabithia Crossword 1 Answer Key

Across
1. Seventh grade bully; ____ Avery
2. Ellie's purchase in Millsburg; see-through _____
7. Worships Jesse; ___ Belle
8. Leslie's parents' jobs
9. Where Leslie's ashes were taken
12. What Miss Edmunds calls Jesse; ____ Kid
14. Jesse needs to pick and can these
15. Burke's have none
16. Eighth grade Aarons daughter
18. Christmas gift to Jesse from Leslie; ___ set
19. Jesse reigned as this over their kingdom
22. Miss Edmunds' favorite song; --- to Be You and Me
24. Fifth grade teacher; ____ Mouth Myers

Down
1. Jesse's youngest sister; ____ Ann
2. Jesse milks her daily; Miss ____
3. Delivers new people to the old Perkins' place
4. Peace-loving music teacher; Miss ____
5. What Leslie calls her parents by; ---- names
6. Secret place
8. Jesse's dad drives there everyday to work; ____ D.C.
9. Author
10. Magical kingdom in C.S. Lewis stories
11. What happened to Jesse's dad (2 words)
13. Leslie's old school
14. May Belle's beloved Christmas gift
17. Jesse's favorite pastime
20. Jesse thinks he has none
21. Local elementary school; ____ Creek
22. Grade Leslie and Jesse were in at Lark Creek
23. Eldest Aarons daughter

Bridge to Terabithia Crossword 2

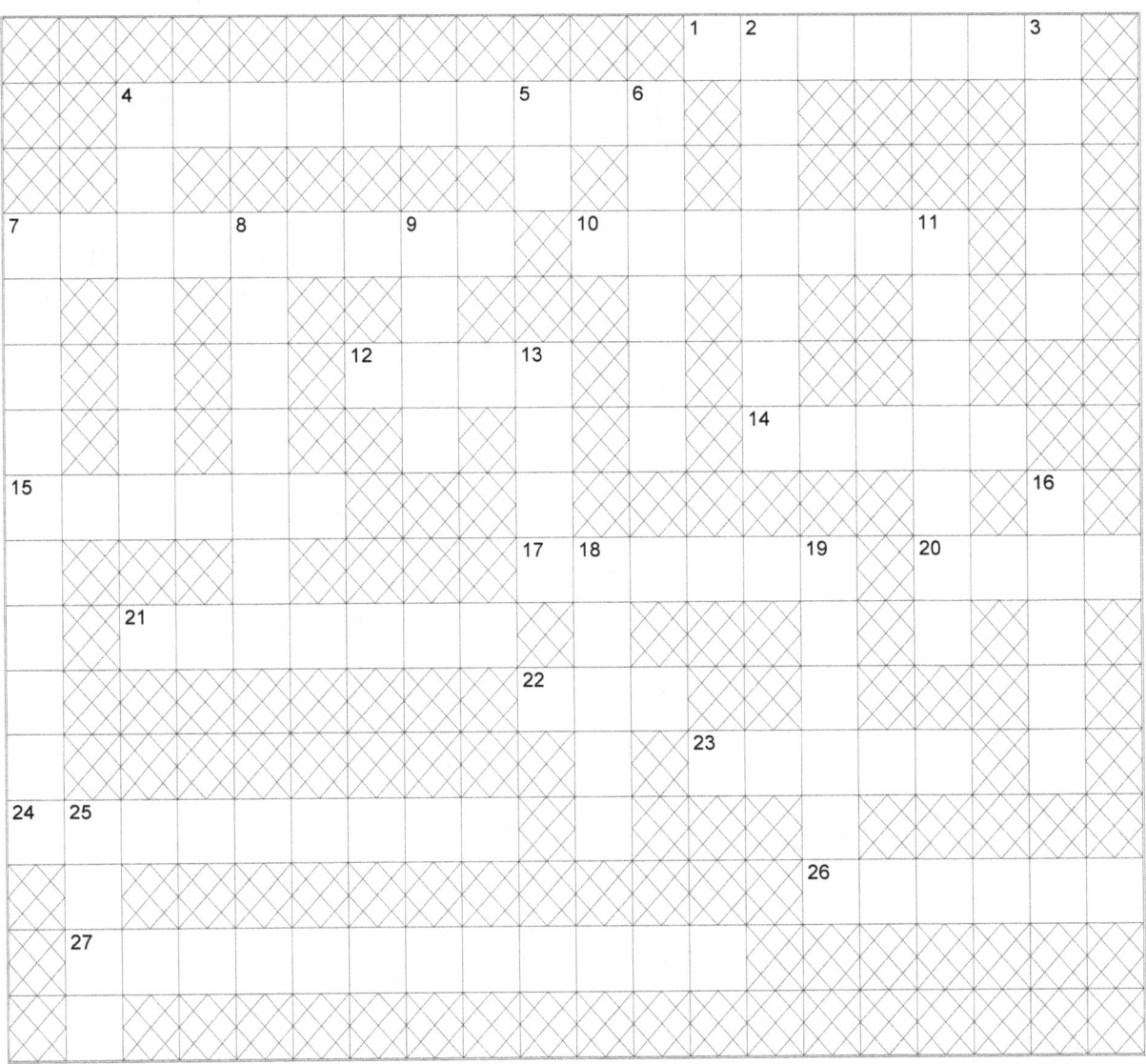

Across
1. Peace-loving music teacher; Miss _____
4. Jesse's dad drives there everyday to work; _____ D.C.
7. Number of students in the fifth-grade class
10. Jesse's favorite pastime
12. Local elementary school; _____ Creek
14. Bribe May Belle took; paper _____
15. Jesse milks her daily; Miss _____
17. Miss Edmunds' instrument
20. Evil curse
21. Fifth grade teacher; _____ Mouth Myers
22. Worships Jesse; _____ Belle
23. Christmas gift to Jesse from Leslie; _____ set
24. Leslie's old school
26. Refinished room of the Burke's; _____ room
27. Where Leslie's ashes were taken

Down
2. How Leslie died
3. Topic of Leslie's essay; _____ diving
4. Leslie's parents' jobs
5. Burke's have none
6. Magical kingdom in C.S. Lewis stories
7. Secret place
8. Guardian of Terabithia; Prince _____
9. What Miss Edmunds calls Jesse; _____ Kid
11. Day trip Miss Edmunds and Jesse take; Nat'l. Art _____
13. Jesse reigned as this over their kingdom
16. Grade Leslie and Jesse were in at Lark Creek
18. Delivers new people to the old Perkins' place
19. Jesse's Christmas gift from his dad; _____ car set
25. Entry into secret kingdom; _____ swing

Bridge to Terabithia Crossword 2 Answer Key

Across
1. Peace-loving music teacher; Miss _____
4. Jesse's dad drives there everyday to work; _____ D.C.
7. Number of students in the fifth-grade class
10. Jesse's favorite pastime
12. Local elementary school; _____ Creek
14. Bribe May Belle took; paper _____
15. Jesse milks her daily; Miss _____
17. Miss Edmunds' instrument
20. Evil curse
21. Fifth grade teacher; _____ Mouth Myers
22. Worships Jesse; _____ Belle
23. Christmas gift to Jesse from Leslie; _____ set
24. Leslie's old school
26. Refinished room of the Burke's; _____ room
27. Where Leslie's ashes were taken

Down
2. How Leslie died
3. Topic of Leslie's essay; _____ diving
4. Leslie's parents' jobs
5. Burke's have none
6. Magical kingdom in C.S. Lewis stories
7. Secret place
8. Guardian of Terabithia; Prince _____
9. What Miss Edmunds calls Jesse; _____ Kid
11. Day trip Miss Edmunds and Jesse take; Nat'l. Art _____
13. Jesse reigned as this over their kingdom
16. Grade Leslie and Jesse were in at Lark Creek
18. Delivers new people to the old Perkins' place
19. Jesse's Christmas gift from his dad; _____ car set
25. Entry into secret kingdom; _____ swing

Bridge to Terabithia Crossword 3

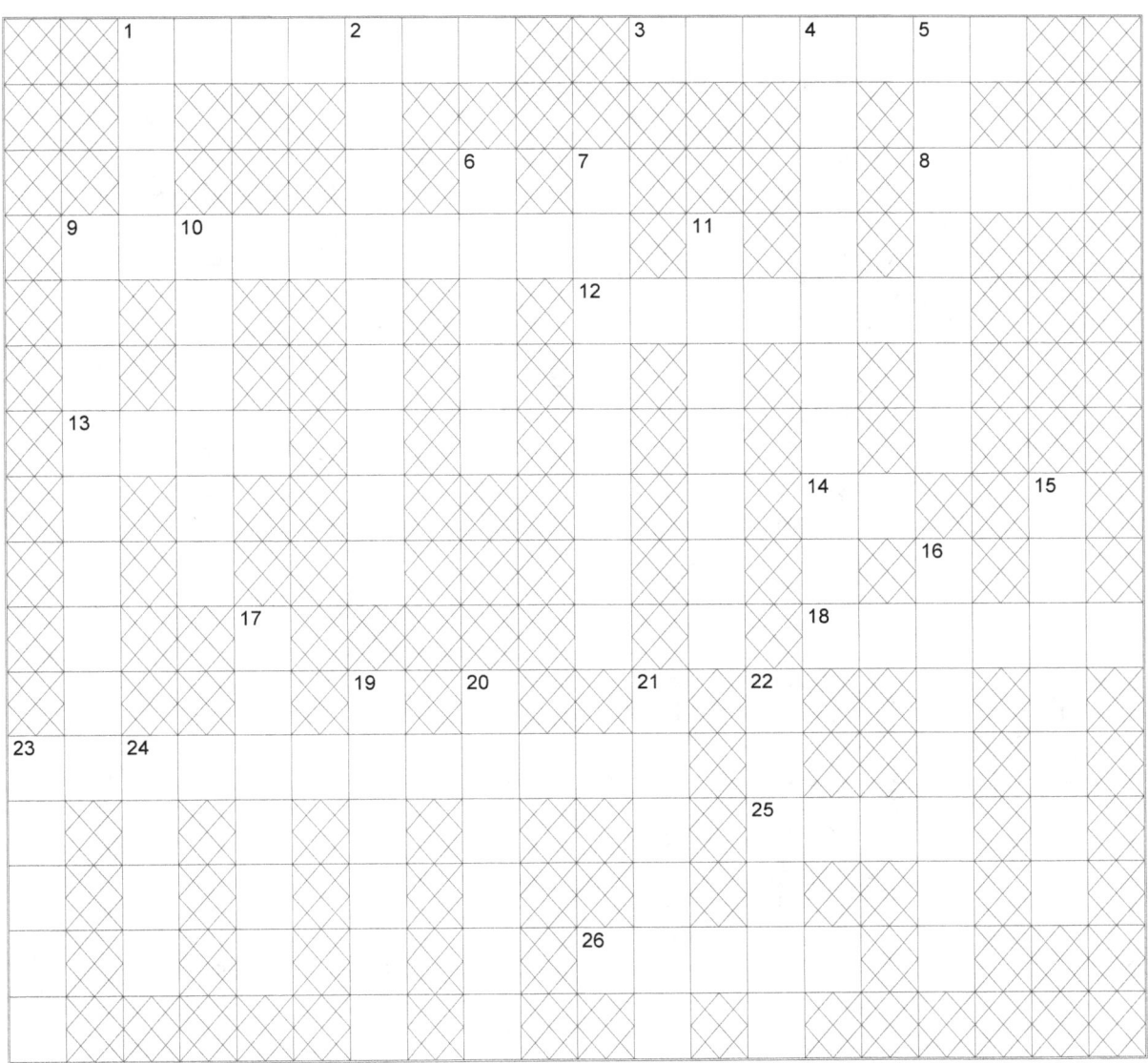

Across
1. Miss Edmunds' day at Lark Creek
3. How Leslie died
8. Worships Jesse; ___ Belle
9. Secret place
12. Guardian of Terabithia; Prince ____
13. Evil curse
14. Burke's have none
18. Magical kingdom in C.S. Lewis stories
23. Where Leslie's ashes were taken
25. Entry into secret kingdom; ____ swing
26. Ten-year-old boy in family of all girls

Down
1. Miss Edmunds' favorite song; --- to Be You and Me
2. Leslie's old school
4. Jesse's dad drives there everyday to work; ____ D.C.
5. Peace-loving music teacher; Miss ____
6. Delivers new people to the old Perkins' place
7. Author
9. Number of students in the fifth-grade class
10. Jesse's Christmas gift from his dad; ___ car set
11. Jesse's favorite pastime
15. What happened to Jesse's dad (2 words)
16. Leslie's parents' jobs
17. Jesse milks her daily; Miss ____
19. Ellie's purchase in Millsburg; see-through _____
20. May Belle's beloved Christmas gift
21. Leslie wanted to go to church with Jesse then
22. Sacred place; Pine _____
23. Christmas gift to Jesse from Leslie; ___ set
24. What Miss Edmunds calls Jesse; ____ Kid

Bridge to Terabithia Crossword 3 Answer Key

	1 F	R	I	2 D	A	Y	S		3 D	R	4 O	W	5 N	E	D
	R			R							W		A		D
	E			L		6 U	7 P				S		8 M	A	Y
9 T	E	10 R	A	B	I	T	H	I	A		11 D		H		U
	H	A		N		A			12 T	E	R	R	I	E	N
	I	C		G		U			E		A		N		D
13 R	A	I	N			T			L		R		G		S
T		N				O			S		I		14 T	V	15 L
Y		G				N			O		N		O		16 W A
O			17 B						N		G		18 N	A R N I A
N			E		19 B	20 B		21 E		22 F		I		D
23 P	24 E	N	N	S	Y	L	V	A	N	I	A		T		O
A	E		S		O		R		A		25 R	O	P	E	F
I	A		I		U		B		S		E		R		F
N	T		E		S		I		26 T	J	E	S	S	E	S
T			E		E				R		T				

Across
1. Miss Edmunds' day at Lark Creek
3. How Leslie died
8. Worships Jesse; ___ Belle
9. Secret place
12. Guardian of Terabithia; Prince ____
13. Evil curse
14. Burke's have none
18. Magical kingdom in C.S. Lewis stories
23. Where Leslie's ashes were taken
25. Entry into secret kingdom; ____ swing
26. Ten-year-old boy in family of all girls

Down
1. Miss Edmunds' favorite song; --- to Be You and Me
2. Leslie's old school
4. Jesse's dad drives there everyday to work; ____ D.C.
5. Peace-loving music teacher; Miss _____
6. Delivers new people to the old Perkins' place
7. Author
9. Number of students in the fifth-grade class
10. Jesse's Christmas gift from his dad; ___ car set
11. Jesse's favorite pastime
15. What happened to Jesse's dad (2 words)
16. Leslie's parents' jobs
17. Jesse milks her daily; Miss ____
19. Ellie's purchase in Millsburg; see-through _____
20. May Belle's beloved Christmas gift
21. Leslie wanted to go to church with Jesse then
22. Sacred place; Pine _____
23. Christmas gift to Jesse from Leslie; ___ set
24. What Miss Edmunds calls Jesse; ____ Kid

Bridge to Terabithia Crossword 4

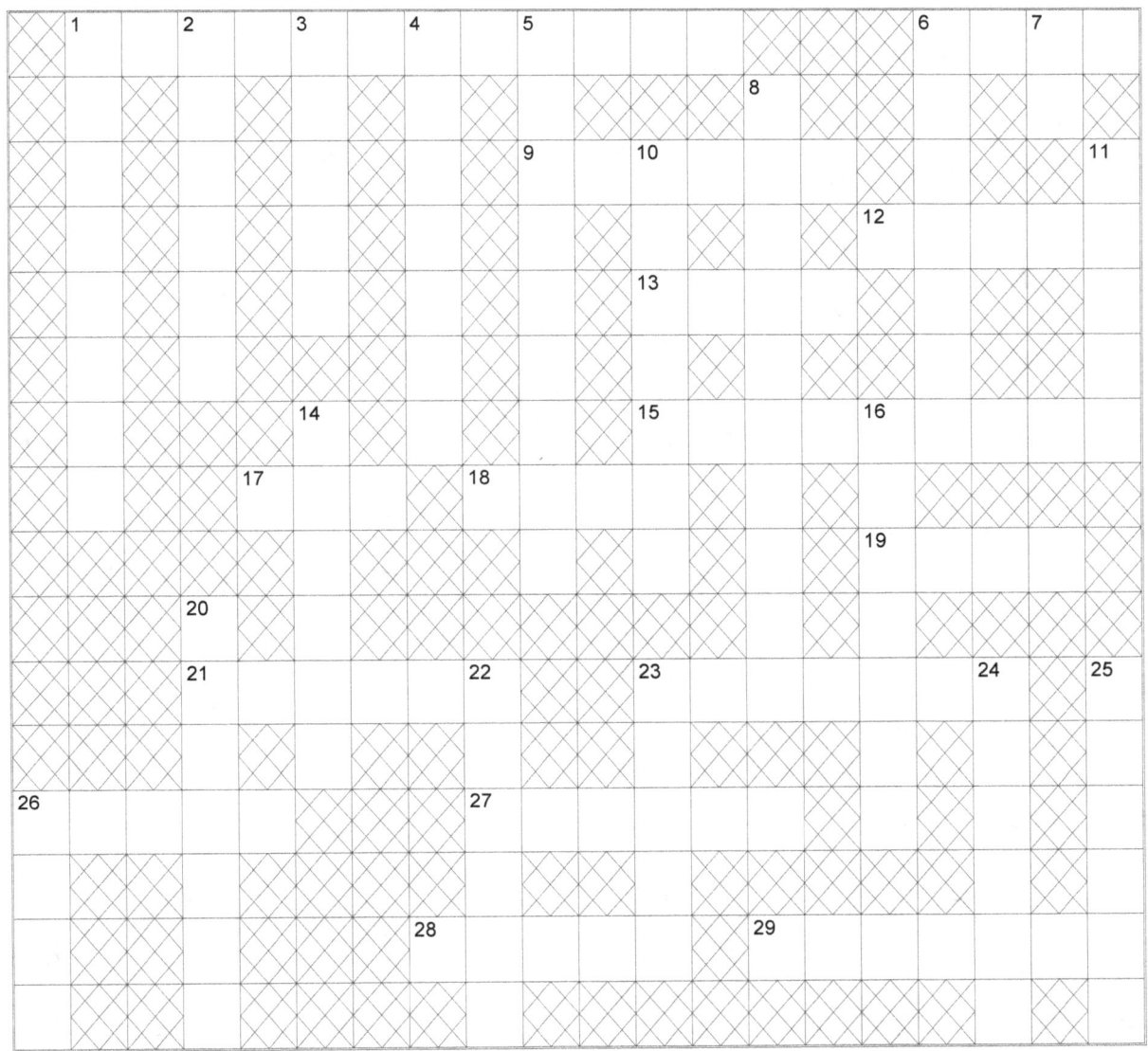

Across
1. Where Leslie's ashes were taken
6. Jesse thinks he has none
9. Used to build bridge over creek bed
12. Eldest Aarons daughter
13. What Miss Edmunds calls Jesse; ____ Kid
15. Number of students in the fifth-grade class
17. Worships Jesse; ___ Belle
18. Entry into secret kingdom; ____ swing
19. Evil curse
21. Jesse's Christmas gift from his dad; ___ car set
23. Jesse's favorite pastime
26. Grade Leslie and Jesse were in at Lark Creek
27. Fastest runner in the fifth grade
28. Jesse needs to pick and can these
29. Miss Edmunds' day at Lark Creek

Down
1. Author
2. Magical kingdom in C.S. Lewis stories
3. Topic of Leslie's essay; ____ diving
4. What happened to Jesse's dad (2 words)
5. Leslie's old school
6. Day trip Miss Edmunds and Jesse take; Nat'l. Art ____
7. Burke's have none
8. Secret place
10. Fifth grade teacher; ____ Mouth Myers
11. Ten-year-old boy in family of all girls
14. Seventh grade bully; ____ Avery
16. Guardian of Terabithia; Prince ____
20. Leslie's parents' jobs
22. Refinished room of the Burke's; ____ room
23. Bribe May Belle took; paper _____
24. Miss Edmunds' instrument
25. Ellie's purchase in Millsburg; see-through _____
26. Miss Edmunds' favorite song; --- to Be You and Me

Bridge to Terabithia Crossword 4 Answer Key

	1 P	2 E	3 N	4 N	5 S	Y	L	V	A	N	I	A		6 G	7 U	T	S
	A	A	C	A	R				8 T					A	V		
	T	R	U	I	9 L	10 U	M	B	E	R			12 E	L	L	11 I	E
	E	N	B	D	I	O			R			13 N	E	A	T		S
	R	I	A	O	N	G			14 S		15 T	H	16 I	R	T	Y	ONE
	S	A		F	F	T		17 M	A	Y	18 R	O	P	E	T	E	
	O	N							N		N	R	H	19 R	A	I	N
	N				20 W	I						O	I	R			
					21 R	A	C	I	N	22 G		23 D	R	A	W	24 I	N	25 G	B
					I	E			O		O		E	U		L
26 F	I	F	T	H			27 L	E	S	L	I	E		N		I	O
R				E			D		L				T		U
E				R		28 B	E	A	N	S		29 F	R	I	D	A	Y	S
E				S			N								R		E

Across

1. Where Leslie's ashes were taken
6. Jesse thinks he has none
9. Used to build bridge over creek bed
12. Eldest Aarons daughter
13. What Miss Edmunds calls Jesse; ____ Kid
15. Number of students in the fifth-grade class
17. Worships Jesse; ___ Belle
18. Entry into secret kingdom; ____ swing
19. Evil curse
21. Jesse's Christmas gift from his dad; ___ car set
23. Jesse's favorite pastime
26. Grade Leslie and Jesse were in at Lark Creek
27. Fastest runner in the fifth grade
28. Jesse needs to pick and can these
29. Miss Edmunds' day at Lark Creek

Down

1. Author
2. Magical kingdom in C.S. Lewis stories
3. Topic of Leslie's essay; ____ diving
4. What happened to Jesse's dad (2 words)
5. Leslie's old school
6. Day trip Miss Edmunds and Jesse take; Nat'l. Art ____
7. Burke's have none
8. Secret place
10. Fifth grade teacher; ____ Mouth Myers
11. Ten-year-old boy in family of all girls
14. Seventh grade bully; ____ Avery
16. Guardian of Terabithia; Prince ____
20. Leslie's parents' jobs
22. Refinished room of the Burke's; ____ room
23. Bribe May Belle took; paper _____
24. Miss Edmunds' instrument
25. Ellie's purchase in Millsburg; see-through _____
26. Miss Edmunds' favorite song; --- to Be You and Me

Bridge to Terabithia

NARNIA	TERABITHIA	BRENDA	RACING	FREE
TERRIEN	MONSTER	ARLINGTON	MAY	PATERSON
VALUE	GEORGIA	FREE SPACE	EDMUNDS	DRAWING
QUEEN	JUDY	LUMBER	TV	JANICE
LESLIE	BESSIE	BARBIE	THIRTYONE	WRITERS

Bridge to Terabithia

FRIDAYS	NEAT	GUTS	GOLDEN	BLOUSE
GALLERY	GUITAR	PENNSYLVANIA	PAINT	JESSE
WASHINGTON	JOYCE	FREE SPACE	BEANS	DROWNED
SCUBA	ROPE	KING	FIRST	FIFTH
ELLIE	EASTER	UHAUL	RAIN	LARK

Bridge to Terabithia

DROWNED	RAIN	BRENDA	FOREST	KING
JANICE	WRITERS	JUDY	TERABITHIA	DRAWING
JOYCE	NEAT	FREE SPACE	DOLLS	PENNSYLVANIA
GUTS	UHAUL	BESSIE	ROPE	FIRST
LESLIE	FIFTH	THIRTYONE	SCUBA	LUMBER

Bridge to Terabithia

WASHINGTON	EDMUNDS	GUITAR	GALLERY	ARLINGTON
VALUE	NARNIA	TV	MONSTER	QUEEN
LAIDOFF	BEANS	FREE SPACE	PATERSON	MAY
RACING	PAINT	LARK	FREE	TERRIEN
FRIDAYS	BLOUSE	EASTER	JESSE	BARBIE

Bridge to Terabithia

ARLINGTON	UHAUL	JESSE	GUITAR	LESLIE
SCUBA	GEORGIA	PAINT	BLOUSE	TV
BESSIE	FIRST	FREE SPACE	EDMUNDS	BRENDA
FOREST	PENNSYLVANIA	DROWNED	GALLERY	KING
DRAWING	LARK	EASTER	BARBIE	MONSTER

Bridge to Terabithia

FREE	MAY	LUMBER	DOLLS	LAIDOFF
RAIN	PATERSON	BEANS	ROPE	WASHINGTON
ELLIE	NEAT	FREE SPACE	FRIDAYS	VALUE
JANICE	GOLDEN	RACING	NARNIA	JUDY
TERABITHIA	THIRTYONE	TERRIEN	GUTS	JOYCE

Bridge to Terabithia

EASTER	ARLINGTON	FREE	SCUBA	TV
BRENDA	BLOUSE	JANICE	VALUE	BESSIE
JESSE	GEORGIA	FREE SPACE	WRITERS	ROPE
JOYCE	GUTS	GOLDEN	LESLIE	GUITAR
RAIN	DRAWING	FIRST	EDMUNDS	FOREST

Bridge to Terabithia

PENNSYLVANIA	ELLIE	PAINT	BARBIE	NARNIA
THIRTYONE	KING	GALLERY	QUEEN	NEAT
FRIDAYS	JUDY	FREE SPACE	TERABITHIA	LUMBER
RACING	DOLLS	LAIDOFF	LARK	DROWNED
MAY	WASHINGTON	FIFTH	BEANS	UHAUL

Bridge to Terabithia

FRIDAYS	PAINT	JOYCE	FIRST	KING
WRITERS	NEAT	RACING	GUTS	FREE
WASHINGTON	NARNIA	FREE SPACE	MAY	SCUBA
TERABITHIA	RAIN	GOLDEN	FOREST	LESLIE
DOLLS	BLOUSE	LAIDOFF	BEANS	PENNSYLVANIA

Bridge to Terabithia

BRENDA	BESSIE	PATERSON	VALUE	TV
FIFTH	LUMBER	QUEEN	GUITAR	GALLERY
ROPE	BARBIE	FREE SPACE	LARK	JUDY
ARLINGTON	MONSTER	EDMUNDS	JESSE	JANICE
ELLIE	UHAUL	DRAWING	THIRTYONE	EASTER

Bridge to Terabithia

PATERSON	EDMUNDS	DRAWING	LARK	FRIDAYS
JOYCE	QUEEN	EASTER	ROPE	GALLERY
FIRST	TV	FREE SPACE	NARNIA	KING
VALUE	WRITERS	PENNSYLVANIA	GUTS	ARLINGTON
UHAUL	RAIN	FIFTH	TERRIEN	NEAT

Bridge to Terabithia

MAY	TERABITHIA	BEANS	JUDY	PAINT
ELLIE	LUMBER	GUITAR	DOLLS	GEORGIA
RACING	BARBIE	FREE SPACE	JESSE	GOLDEN
BESSIE	DROWNED	FOREST	LESLIE	BRENDA
FREE	MONSTER	SCUBA	THIRTYONE	BLOUSE

Bridge to Terabithia

PATERSON	TV	TERRIEN	PENNSYLVANIA	MONSTER
RAIN	SCUBA	FIRST	GOLDEN	JOYCE
JANICE	ELLIE	FREE SPACE	MAY	THIRTYONE
NARNIA	ARLINGTON	UHAUL	GEORGIA	BEANS
DOLLS	QUEEN	BARBIE	EDMUNDS	PAINT

Bridge to Terabithia

LAIDOFF	BRENDA	NEAT	FRIDAYS	FREE
EASTER	ROPE	BLOUSE	FOREST	GUTS
BESSIE	RACING	FREE SPACE	GALLERY	WRITERS
TERABITHIA	FIFTH	JUDY	DRAWING	WASHINGTON
JESSE	LARK	GUITAR	LUMBER	DROWNED

Bridge to Terabithia

JUDY	DROWNED	ELLIE	ARLINGTON	BRENDA
JOYCE	LESLIE	DRAWING	MONSTER	LUMBER
TV	FREE	FREE SPACE	VALUE	FIFTH
LAIDOFF	WASHINGTON	BLOUSE	PATERSON	GUTS
BEANS	KING	ROPE	PENNSYLVANIA	FIRST

Bridge to Terabithia

TERRIEN	GEORGIA	JANICE	LARK	JESSE
UHAUL	NEAT	PAINT	THIRTYONE	MAY
RAIN	EDMUNDS	FREE SPACE	TERABITHIA	BARBIE
NARNIA	GUITAR	SCUBA	FRIDAYS	BESSIE
DOLLS	WRITERS	GOLDEN	FOREST	RACING

Bridge to Terabithia

EASTER	JESSE	GUTS	NEAT	RACING
RAIN	ROPE	BESSIE	PENNSYLVANIA	FIRST
THIRTYONE	EDMUNDS	FREE SPACE	VALUE	LARK
WASHINGTON	LESLIE	ELLIE	JOYCE	BEANS
PATERSON	GUITAR	GEORGIA	NARNIA	MAY

Bridge to Terabithia

TERABITHIA	TV	UHAUL	GALLERY	JANICE
DROWNED	ARLINGTON	WRITERS	MONSTER	QUEEN
FOREST	KING	FREE SPACE	BARBIE	FIFTH
GOLDEN	FRIDAYS	BRENDA	JUDY	SCUBA
FREE	LUMBER	DOLLS	TERRIEN	DRAWING

Bridge to Terabithia

DROWNED	LUMBER	ROPE	JANICE	GUITAR
QUEEN	ELLIE	TERRIEN	TV	JOYCE
PENNSYLVANIA	GOLDEN	FREE SPACE	NARNIA	BLOUSE
FIRST	PATERSON	VALUE	DOLLS	TERABITHIA
WRITERS	BEANS	FREE	GEORGIA	BRENDA

Bridge to Terabithia

PAINT	NEAT	MONSTER	EASTER	BARBIE
BESSIE	ARLINGTON	MAY	WASHINGTON	UHAUL
KING	FOREST	FREE SPACE	JESSE	SCUBA
LESLIE	RAIN	LAIDOFF	DRAWING	GUTS
FIFTH	GALLERY	RACING	LARK	FRIDAYS

Bridge to Terabithia

RACING	JESSE	TERRIEN	QUEEN	THIRTYONE
GUTS	JOYCE	RAIN	LARK	ELLIE
EDMUNDS	DRAWING	FREE SPACE	BLOUSE	GEORGIA
DROWNED	JANICE	WASHINGTON	MAY	BESSIE
BARBIE	GALLERY	FREE	FIFTH	FRIDAYS

Bridge to Terabithia

TERABITHIA	PAINT	TV	FIRST	BEANS
WRITERS	NEAT	GOLDEN	GUITAR	PENNSYLVANIA
BRENDA	JUDY	FREE SPACE	DOLLS	UHAUL
ARLINGTON	LESLIE	MONSTER	LUMBER	NARNIA
LAIDOFF	PATERSON	VALUE	KING	ROPE

Bridge to Terabithia

FIRST	DROWNED	DOLLS	FIFTH	RACING
QUEEN	GALLERY	RAIN	JOYCE	FRIDAYS
THIRTYONE	WRITERS	FREE SPACE	FREE	ELLIE
ROPE	GEORGIA	JANICE	PENNSYLVANIA	NARNIA
LUMBER	BEANS	PAINT	UHAUL	EDMUNDS

Bridge to Terabithia

LAIDOFF	TERRIEN	ARLINGTON	BARBIE	EASTER
TERABITHIA	PATERSON	FOREST	DRAWING	WASHINGTON
MAY	KING	FREE SPACE	SCUBA	VALUE
GUTS	BLOUSE	NEAT	TV	GOLDEN
JUDY	MONSTER	BRENDA	GUITAR	LESLIE

Bridge to Terabithia

DOLLS	ELLIE	MONSTER	NARNIA	FREE
EDMUNDS	KING	BESSIE	GUTS	JANICE
FIFTH	LESLIE	FREE SPACE	THIRTYONE	GUITAR
GALLERY	FOREST	NEAT	JOYCE	TV
BARBIE	SCUBA	VALUE	ARLINGTON	DROWNED

Bridge to Terabithia

MAY	FRIDAYS	FIRST	PENNSYLVANIA	UHAUL
LAIDOFF	GEORGIA	QUEEN	EASTER	TERRIEN
GOLDEN	RACING	FREE SPACE	JUDY	BRENDA
PAINT	PATERSON	BEANS	BLOUSE	WRITERS
JESSE	ROPE	WASHINGTON	LUMBER	TERABITHIA

Copyrighted

Bridge to Terabithia

RACING	VALUE	JUDY	SCUBA	GALLERY
THIRTYONE	DOLLS	LUMBER	FRIDAYS	WRITERS
EDMUNDS	JESSE	FREE SPACE	ELLIE	WASHINGTON
GUTS	BLOUSE	BARBIE	MAY	GEORGIA
TERABITHIA	ARLINGTON	FOREST	RAIN	FREE

Bridge to Terabithia

PATERSON	ROPE	PAINT	FIFTH	NEAT
BESSIE	NARNIA	LARK	GUITAR	TV
JANICE	BEANS	FREE SPACE	MONSTER	GOLDEN
KING	TERRIEN	BRENDA	DRAWING	JOYCE
EASTER	QUEEN	LESLIE	PENNSYLVANIA	DROWNED

Bridge to Terabithia

FOREST	RACING	ROPE	JANICE	FRIDAYS
BLOUSE	PATERSON	GUTS	BRENDA	WASHINGTON
NEAT	MAY	FREE SPACE	GOLDEN	UHAUL
VALUE	DRAWING	LAIDOFF	ARLINGTON	FREE
DOLLS	TERABITHIA	NARNIA	QUEEN	TERRIEN

Bridge to Terabithia

GALLERY	BEANS	GEORGIA	EDMUNDS	SCUBA
JUDY	THIRTYONE	BESSIE	LUMBER	FIRST
TV	RAIN	FREE SPACE	EASTER	BARBIE
MONSTER	JOYCE	GUITAR	FIFTH	LESLIE
LARK	ELLIE	WRITERS	PAINT	KING

Bridge to Terabithia

GUITAR	FREE	PENNSYLVANIA	TV	ELLIE
SCUBA	VALUE	JUDY	QUEEN	ROPE
MAY	LARK	FREE SPACE	GEORGIA	EDMUNDS
NEAT	THIRTYONE	PATERSON	TERABITHIA	FIFTH
BESSIE	DRAWING	RAIN	NARNIA	JESSE

Bridge to Terabithia

RACING	FOREST	BRENDA	LAIDOFF	BARBIE
JANICE	GUTS	ARLINGTON	WASHINGTON	LUMBER
BLOUSE	DOLLS	FREE SPACE	LESLIE	KING
WRITERS	MONSTER	JOYCE	DROWNED	GALLERY
FIRST	TERRIEN	FRIDAYS	BEANS	EASTER

Bridge To Terabithia Vocabulary Word List

No.	Word	Clue/Definition
1.	ACCUSATION	Guilty charge
2.	ALCOVE	Recessed opening
3.	CAGEY	Tricky; sly
4.	COMMEND	Entrust; commit
5.	COMPLACENT	Self-satisfied
6.	CONSOLATION	Comfort
7.	CONSOLIDATED	Conbimed
8.	CONSPIRING	Plotting
9.	CONSTRICTING	Tightening
10.	CRIMSON	Deep red
11.	DELIBERATELY	On purpose; intentionally
12.	DELICATELY	Sissified manner
13.	DESPERATE	Hopeless
14.	DESPISING	Hating
15.	DESPITE	In spite of
16.	DISCERN	See; recognize
17.	DOUSED	Drenched; soaked
18.	DREAD	Terror
19.	DREDGING	Bringing to the surface
20.	DREGS	Remains
21.	EXHILARATION	Thrill
22.	FALTERED	Hesitated; wavered
23.	FOUNDLING	Abandoned infant
24.	GARISH	Glaring; showy
25.	GRIT	Backbone
26.	HYPOCRIITICAL	Two-faced
27.	INCLINED	Known to; tendency
28.	INSUFFICIENCIES	Weaknesses
29.	INTOXICATED	Drunk
30.	MOURNING	Grieving
31.	MUDDLED	Confused
32.	NAUSEATINGLY	Sickeningly
33.	OBLIGED	Grateful
34.	OMINOUSLY	Threateningly; darkly
35.	PANDEMONIUM	Uproar
36.	PARAMEDICS	Emergency medical persons
37.	PARAPETS	Barriers
38.	PITEOUSLY	Pitifully
39.	PREDATORS	Those who live by preying on others
40.	PRESCRIBED	Assigned; designated
41.	PROVERBIAL	Obvious
42.	PUDGY	Chubby
43.	REGALLY	Stately; dignified
44.	REGICIDE	The killing of a king
45.	RELENTLESSLY	Without stopping
46.	RELUCTANT	Unwilling
47.	REPENTED	Took back; changed for the better
48.	RETRIEVED	Found; recovered
49.	REVENGE	To get back at; punishment
50.	SANCTUARY	Place of worship
51.	SHEBANG	The whole thing

Bridge To Terabithia Vocabulary Word List Continued

No.	Word	Clue/Definition
52.	SOLEMN	Serious
53.	SPECTACLE	Public display
54.	SPECULATION	Consideration; thought
55.	SPORADICALLY	Occasionally
56.	SURPLUS	Extra amount
57.	TRAITOROUS	Disloyal; back-stabbing
58.	VANQUISHED	Defeated
59.	VIGOROUSLY	Energetically
60.	VILE	Mean; disgusting

Bridge to Terabithia Vocabulary Fil In The Blank 1

_____ 1. Consideration; thought
_____ 2. Pitifully
_____ 3. Uproar
_____ 4. Those who live by preying on others
_____ 5. Backbone
_____ 6. Glaring; showy
_____ 7. Thrill
_____ 8. See; recognize
_____ 9. Guilty charge
_____ 10. Tightening
_____ 11. Mean; disgusting
_____ 12. Chubby
_____ 13. Conbimed
_____ 14. Weaknesses
_____ 15. Plotting
_____ 16. Terror
_____ 17. Threateningly; darkly
_____ 18. Obvious
_____ 19. Two-faced
_____ 20. In spite of

Bridge to Terabithia Vocabulary Fill In The Blank 1 Answer Key

SPECULATION	1. Consideration; thought
PITEOUSLY	2. Pitifully
PANDEMONIUM	3. Uproar
PREDATORS	4. Those who live by preying on others
GRIT	5. Backbone
GARISH	6. Glaring; showy
EXHILARATION	7. Thrill
DISCERN	8. See; recognize
ACCUSATION	9. Guilty charge
CONSTRICTING	10. Tightening
VILE	11. Mean; disgusting
PUDGY	12. Chubby
CONSOLIDATED	13. Conbimed
INSUFFICIENCIES	14. Weaknesses
CONSPIRING	15. Plotting
DREAD	16. Terror
OMINOUSLY	17. Threateningly; darkly
PROVERBIAL	18. Obvious
HYPOCRIITICAL	19. Two-faced
DESPITE	20. In spite of

Bridge to Terabithia Vocabulary Fill In The Blank 2

_____ 1. Deep red

_____ 2. Remains

_____ 3. Occasionally

_____ 4. Comfort

_____ 5. Hesitated; wavered

_____ 6. Known to; tendency

_____ 7. The killing of a king

_____ 8. Those who live by preying on others

_____ 9. Self-satisfied

_____ 10. Weaknesses

_____ 11. Plotting

_____ 12. Abandoned infant

_____ 13. Guilty charge

_____ 14. Hating

_____ 15. Uproar

_____ 16. Public display

_____ 17. Recessed opening

_____ 18. Terror

_____ 19. Mean; disgusting

_____ 20. Two-faced

Bridge to Terabithia Vocabulary Fill In The Blank 2 Answer Key

CRIMSON	1. Deep red
DREGS	2. Remains
SPORADICALLY	3. Occasionally
CONSOLATION	4. Comfort
FALTERED	5. Hesitated; wavered
INCLINED	6. Known to; tendency
REGICIDE	7. The killing of a king
PREDATORS	8. Those who live by preying on others
COMPLACENT	9. Self-satisfied
INSUFFICIENCIES	10. Weaknesses
CONSPIRING	11. Plotting
FOUNDLING	12. Abandoned infant
ACCUSATION	13. Guilty charge
DESPISING	14. Hating
PANDEMONIUM	15. Uproar
SPECTACLE	16. Public display
ALCOVE	17. Recessed opening
DREAD	18. Terror
VILE	19. Mean; disgusting
HYPOCRIITICAL	20. Two-faced

Bridge to Terabithia Vocablary Fill In The Blank 3

_____ 1. Hopeless
_____ 2. Extra amount
_____ 3. Consideration; thought
_____ 4. Sissified manner
_____ 5. Serious
_____ 6. Two-faced
_____ 7. On purpose; intentionally
_____ 8. Stately; dignified
_____ 9. Found; recovered
_____ 10. Glaring; showy
_____ 11. Defeated
_____ 12. Remains
_____ 13. Obvious
_____ 14. Uproar
_____ 15. Entrust; commit
_____ 16. Grateful
_____ 17. Without stopping
_____ 18. Tricky; sly
_____ 19. Public display
_____ 20. Assigned; designated

Bridge to Terabithia Vocabulary Fill In The Blank 3 Answer Key

DESPERATE	1. Hopeless
SURPLUS	2. Extra amount
SPECULATION	3. Consideration; thought
DELICATELY	4. Sissified manner
SOLEMN	5. Serious
HYPOCRIITICAL	6. Two-faced
DELIBERATELY	7. On purpose; intentionally
REGALLY	8. Stately; dignified
RETRIEVED	9. Found; recovered
GARISH	10. Glaring; showy
VANQUISHED	11. Defeated
DREGS	12. Remains
PROVERBIAL	13. Obvious
PANDEMONIUM	14. Uproar
COMMEND	15. Entrust; commit
OBLIGED	16. Grateful
RELENTLESSLY	17. Without stopping
CAGEY	18. Tricky; sly
SPECTACLE	19. Public display
PRESCRIBED	20. Assigned; designated

Bridge to Terabithia Vocabulary Fill In The Blank 4

_____ 1. See; recognize

_____ 2. Unwilling

_____ 3. Tightening

_____ 4. Weaknesses

_____ 5. Threateningly; darkly

_____ 6. Grateful

_____ 7. Barriers

_____ 8. Defeated

_____ 9. The whole thing

_____ 10. Hesitated; wavered

_____ 11. To get back at; punishment

_____ 12. The killing of a king

_____ 13. Disloyal; back-stabbing

_____ 14. Entrust; commit

_____ 15. Assigned; designated

_____ 16. Hopeless

_____ 17. Drenched; soaked

_____ 18. Grieving

_____ 19. Confused

_____ 20. Bringing to the surface

Bridge to Terabithia Vocabulary Fill In The Blank 4 Answer Key

DISCERN	1. See; recognize
RELUCTANT	2. Unwilling
CONSTRICTING	3. Tightening
INSUFFICIENCIES	4. Weaknesses
OMINOUSLY	5. Threateningly; darkly
OBLIGED	6. Grateful
PARAPETS	7. Barriers
VANQUISHED	8. Defeated
SHEBANG	9. The whole thing
FALTERED	10. Hesitated; wavered
REVENGE	11. To get back at; punishment
REGICIDE	12. The killing of a king
TRAITOROUS	13. Disloyal; back-stabbing
COMMEND	14. Entrust; commit
PRESCRIBED	15. Assigned; designated
DESPERATE	16. Hopeless
DOUSED	17. Drenched; soaked
MOURNING	18. Grieving
MUDDLED	19. Confused
DREDGING	20. Bringing to the surface

Bridge to Terabithia Vocabulary Matching 1

___ 1. INTOXICATED   A. Known to; tendency
___ 2. SOLEMN   B. Tricky; sly
___ 3. DESPISING   C. Emergency medical persons
___ 4. OBLIGED   D. In spite of
___ 5. DELIBERATELY   E. Guilty charge
___ 6. PITEOUSLY   F. Barriers
___ 7. RELUCTANT   G. Assigned; designated
___ 8. ACCUSATION   H. Defeated
___ 9. REPENTED   I. Plotting
___10. SHEBANG   J. Hating
___11. COMMEND   K. Entrust; commit
___12. DESPITE   L. Drunk
___13. INSUFFICIENCIES   M. Backbone
___14. PARAPETS   N. Weaknesses
___15. PRESCRIBED   O. On purpose; intentionally
___16. VANQUISHED   P. The whole thing
___17. CONSPIRING   Q. The killing of a king
___18. REVENGE   R. Unwilling
___19. REGICIDE   S. Sickeningly
___20. GRIT   T. Pitifully
___21. PARAMEDICS   U. Hesitated; wavered
___22. CAGEY   V. Took back; changed for the better
___23. NAUSEATINGLY   W. Grateful
___24. INCLINED   X. Serious
___25. FALTERED   Y. To get back at; punishment

Copyrighted

Bridge to Terabithia Vocabulary Matching 1 Answer Key

L - 1. INTOXICATED	A. Known to; tendency
X - 2. SOLEMN	B. Tricky; sly
J - 3. DESPISING	C. Emergency medical persons
W - 4. OBLIGED	D. In spite of
O - 5. DELIBERATELY	E. Guilty charge
T - 6. PITEOUSLY	F. Barriers
R - 7. RELUCTANT	G. Assigned; designated
E - 8. ACCUSATION	H. Defeated
V - 9. REPENTED	I. Plotting
P - 10. SHEBANG	J. Hating
K - 11. COMMEND	K. Entrust; commit
D - 12. DESPITE	L. Drunk
N - 13. INSUFFICIENCIES	M. Backbone
F - 14. PARAPETS	N. Weaknesses
G - 15. PRESCRIBED	O. On purpose; intentionally
H - 16. VANQUISHED	P. The whole thing
I - 17. CONSPIRING	Q. The killing of a king
Y - 18. REVENGE	R. Unwilling
Q - 19. REGICIDE	S. Sickeningly
M - 20. GRIT	T. Pitifully
C - 21. PARAMEDICS	U. Hesitated; wavered
B - 22. CAGEY	V. Took back; changed for the better
S - 23. NAUSEATINGLY	W. Grateful
A - 24. INCLINED	X. Serious
U - 25. FALTERED	Y. To get back at; punishment

Bridge to Terabithia Vocabulary Matching 2

___ 1. PARAMEDICS   A. Guilty charge
___ 2. ACCUSATION   B. Obvious
___ 3. GARISH   C. The whole thing
___ 4. DISCERN   D. Tightening
___ 5. FALTERED   E. Place of worship
___ 6. PITEOUSLY   F. Without stopping
___ 7. CAGEY   G. Took back; changed for the better
___ 8. DESPITE   H. Bringing to the surface
___ 9. DOUSED   I. To get back at; punishment
___ 10. CONSTRICTING   J. Tricky; sly
___ 11. DREAD   K. Drenched; soaked
___ 12. DELIBERATELY   L. See; recognize
___ 13. SANCTUARY   M. Pitifully
___ 14. RELUCTANT   N. Emergency medical persons
___ 15. PROVERBIAL   O. Weaknesses
___ 16. SHEBANG   P. Glaring; showy
___ 17. DREDGING   Q. Unwilling
___ 18. REVENGE   R. Terror
___ 19. RELENTLESSLY   S. In spite of
___ 20. REPENTED   T. Recessed opening
___ 21. TRAITOROUS   U. Disloyal; back-stabbing
___ 22. REGICIDE   V. The killing of a king
___ 23. ALCOVE   W. Threateningly; darkly
___ 24. OMINOUSLY   X. Hesitated; wavered
___ 25. INSUFFICIENCIES   Y. On purpose; intentionally

Bridge to Terabithia Vocabulary Matching 2 Answer Key

N - 1. PARAMEDICS	A.	Guilty charge
A - 2. ACCUSATION	B.	Obvious
P - 3. GARISH	C.	The whole thing
L - 4. DISCERN	D.	Tightening
X - 5. FALTERED	E.	Place of worship
M - 6. PITEOUSLY	F.	Without stopping
J - 7. CAGEY	G.	Took back; changed for the better
S - 8. DESPITE	H.	Bringing to the surface
K - 9. DOUSED	I.	To get back at; punishment
D - 10. CONSTRICTING	J.	Tricky; sly
R - 11. DREAD	K.	Drenched; soaked
Y - 12. DELIBERATELY	L.	See; recognize
E - 13. SANCTUARY	M.	Pitifully
Q - 14. RELUCTANT	N.	Emergency medical persons
B - 15. PROVERBIAL	O.	Weaknesses
C - 16. SHEBANG	P.	Glaring; showy
H - 17. DREDGING	Q.	Unwilling
I - 18. REVENGE	R.	Terror
F - 19. RELENTLESSLY	S.	In spite of
G - 20. REPENTED	T.	Recessed opening
U - 21. TRAITOROUS	U.	Disloyal; back-stabbing
V - 22. REGICIDE	V.	The killing of a king
T - 23. ALCOVE	W.	Threateningly; darkly
W - 24. OMINOUSLY	X.	Hesitated; wavered
O - 25. INSUFFICIENCIES	Y.	On purpose; intentionally

Bridge to Terabithia Vocabulary Matching 3

___ 1. PIteously   A. Obvious
___ 2. REGALLY   B. Took back; changed for the better
___ 3. DELICATELY   C. Sissified manner
___ 4. VIGOROUSLY   D. Pitifully
___ 5. DESPISING   E. Disloyal; back-stabbing
___ 6. TRAITOROUS   F. Deep red
___ 7. DESPERATE   G. Hopeless
___ 8. OMINOUSLY   H. Energetically
___ 9. CONSTRICTING   I. In spite of
___10. CAGEY   J. Drenched; soaked
___11. RELENTLESSLY   K. See; recognize
___12. REPENTED   L. Recessed opening
___13. DISCERN   M. Those who live by preying on others
___14. RELUCTANT   N. Tightening
___15. INCLINED   O. Known to; tendency
___16. SPORADICALLY   P. Tricky; sly
___17. PROVERBIAL   Q. Threateningly; darkly
___18. DOUSED   R. Unwilling
___19. CRIMSON   S. Remains
___20. DREGS   T. Occasionally
___21. DESPITE   U. Without stopping
___22. PREDATORS   V. Glaring; showy
___23. MOURNING   W. Hating
___24. GARISH   X. Stately; dignified
___25. ALCOVE   Y. Grieving

Bridge to Terabithia Vocabulary Matching 3 Answer Key

D - 1. PITEOUSLY	A.	Obvious
X - 2. REGALLY	B.	Took back; changed for the better
C - 3. DELICATELY	C.	Sissified manner
H - 4. VIGOROUSLY	D.	Pitifully
W - 5. DESPISING	E.	Disloyal; back-stabbing
E - 6. TRAITOROUS	F.	Deep red
G - 7. DESPERATE	G.	Hopeless
Q - 8. OMINOUSLY	H.	Energetically
N - 9. CONSTRICTING	I.	In spite of
P - 10. CAGEY	J.	Drenched; soaked
U - 11. RELENTLESSLY	K.	See; recognize
B - 12. REPENTED	L.	Recessed opening
K - 13. DISCERN	M.	Those who live by preying on others
R - 14. RELUCTANT	N.	Tightening
O - 15. INCLINED	O.	Known to; tendency
T - 16. SPORADICALLY	P.	Tricky; sly
A - 17. PROVERBIAL	Q.	Threateningly; darkly
J - 18. DOUSED	R.	Unwilling
F - 19. CRIMSON	S.	Remains
S - 20. DREGS	T.	Occasionally
I - 21. DESPITE	U.	Without stopping
M - 22. PREDATORS	V.	Glaring; showy
Y - 23. MOURNING	W.	Hating
V - 24. GARISH	X.	Stately; dignified
L - 25. ALCOVE	Y.	Grieving

Bridge to Terabithia Vocabulary Matching 4

___ 1. TRAITOROUS   A. Serious
___ 2. CONSOLIDATED   B. Comfort
___ 3. DESPISING   C. Public display
___ 4. PANDEMONIUM   D. Two-faced
___ 5. COMMEND   E. Without stopping
___ 6. MUDDLED   F. Mean; disgusting
___ 7. SHEBANG   G. The whole thing
___ 8. DELICATELY   H. Drunk
___ 9. SOLEMN   I. Guilty charge
___10. VILE   J. Abandoned infant
___11. CONSOLATION   K. Emergency medical persons
___12. OBLIGED   L. Uproar
___13. INTOXICATED   M. Place of worship
___14. VANQUISHED   N. Sissified manner
___15. CRIMSON   O. Energetically
___16. ACCUSATION   P. Hating
___17. SURPLUS   Q. Extra amount
___18. PARAMEDICS   R. Barriers
___19. RELENTLESSLY   S. Confused
___20. HYPOCRIITICAL   T. Grateful
___21. VIGOROUSLY   U. Conbimed
___22. SANCTUARY   V. Entrust; commit
___23. PARAPETS   W. Defeated
___24. SPECTACLE   X. Disloyal; back-stabbing
___25. FOUNDLING   Y. Deep red

Bridge to Terabithia Vocabulary Matching 4 Answer Key

X - 1. TRAITOROUS	A.	Serious
U - 2. CONSOLIDATED	B.	Comfort
P - 3. DESPISING	C.	Public display
L - 4. PANDEMONIUM	D.	Two-faced
V - 5. COMMEND	E.	Without stopping
S - 6. MUDDLED	F.	Mean; disgusting
G - 7. SHEBANG	G.	The whole thing
N - 8. DELICATELY	H.	Drunk
A - 9. SOLEMN	I.	Guilty charge
F - 10. VILE	J.	Abandoned infant
B - 11. CONSOLATION	K.	Emergency medical persons
T - 12. OBLIGED	L.	Uproar
H - 13. INTOXICATED	M.	Place of worship
W - 14. VANQUISHED	N.	Sissified manner
Y - 15. CRIMSON	O.	Energetically
I - 16. ACCUSATION	P.	Hating
Q - 17. SURPLUS	Q.	Extra amount
K - 18. PARAMEDICS	R.	Barriers
E - 19. RELENTLESSLY	S.	Confused
D - 20. HYPOCRIITICAL	T.	Grateful
O - 21. VIGOROUSLY	U.	Conbimed
M - 22. SANCTUARY	V.	Entrust; commit
R - 23. PARAPETS	W.	Defeated
C - 24. SPECTACLE	X.	Disloyal; back-stabbing
J - 25. FOUNDLING	Y.	Deep red

Bridge to Terabithia Vocabulary Magic Squares 1

Match the definition with the vocabulary word. Put your answers in the magic squares below. When your answers are correct, all columns and rows will add to the same number.

A. DREDGING
B. DELIBERATELY
C. DESPISING
D. FALTERED
E. ALCOVE
F. CONSTRICTING
G. SPORADICALLY
H. COMPLACENT
I. PITEOUSLY
J. PRESCRIBED
K. SPECULATION
L. SHEBANG
M. GRIT
N. SANCTUARY
O. RELENTLESSLY
P. TRAITOROUS

1. Hating
2. Assigned; designated
3. Tightening
4. Without stopping
5. Disloyal; back-stabbing
6. Recessed opening
7. Pitifully
8. Hesitated; wavered
9. Backbone
10. Self-satisfied
11. The whole thing
12. Bringing to the surface
13. On purpose; intentionally
14. Consideration; thought
15. Occasionally
16. Place of worship

A=	B=	C=	D=
E=	F=	G=	H=
I=	J=	K=	L=
M=	N=	O=	P=

Bridge to Terabithia Vocabulary Magic Squares 1 Answer Key

Match the definition with the vocabulary word. Put your answers in the magic squares below. When your answers are correct, all columns and rows will add to the same number.

A. DREDGING
B. DELIBERATELY
C. DESPISING
D. FALTERED
E. ALCOVE
F. CONSTRICTING
G. SPORADICALLY
H. COMPLACENT
I. PITEOUSLY
J. PRESCRIBED
K. SPECULATION
L. SHEBANG
M. GRIT
N. SANCTUARY
O. RELENTLESSLY
P. TRAITOROUS

1. Hating
2. Assigned; designated
3. Tightening
4. Without stopping
5. Disloyal; back-stabbing
6. Recessed opening
7. Pitifully
8. Hesitated; wavered
9. Backbone
10. Self-satisfied
11. The whole thing
12. Bringing to the surface
13. On purpose; intentionally
14. Consideration; thought
15. Occasionally
16. Place of worship

A=12	B=13	C=1	D=8
E=6	F=3	G=15	H=10
I=7	J=2	K=14	L=11
M=9	N=16	O=4	P=5

Bridge to Terabithia Vocabulary Magic Squares 2

Match the definition with the vocabulary word. Put your answers in the magic squares below. When your answers are correct, all columns and rows will add to the same number.

A. VILE
B. PARAMEDICS
C. RELUCTANT
D. CRIMSON
E. MOURNING
F. DELICATELY
G. PREDATORS
H. DOUSED
I. GARISH
J. COMMEND
K. REGICIDE
L. DREDGING
M. NAUSEATINGLY
N. COMPLACENT
O. ALCOVE
P. VIGOROUSLY

1. Sissified manner
2. Glaring; showy
3. Recessed opening
4. Deep red
5. Sickeningly
6. Emergency medical persons
7. Drenched; soaked
8. The killing of a king
9. Unwilling
10. Energetically
11. Entrust; commit
12. Grieving
13. Bringing to the surface
14. Those who live by preying on others
15. Mean; disgusting
16. Self-satisfied

A=	B=	C=	D=
E=	F=	G=	H=
I=	J=	K=	L=
M=	N=	O=	P=

Bridge to Terabithia Vocabulay Magic Squares 2 Answer Key

Match the definition with the vocabulary word. Put your answers in the magic squares below. When your answers are correct, all columns and rows will add to the same number.

A. VILE
B. PARAMEDICS
C. RELUCTANT
D. CRIMSON
E. MOURNING
F. DELICATELY
G. PREDATORS
H. DOUSED
I. GARISH
J. COMMEND
K. REGICIDE
L. DREDGING
M. NAUSEATINGLY
N. COMPLACENT
O. ALCOVE
P. VIGOROUSLY

1. Sissified manner
2. Glaring; showy
3. Recessed opening
4. Deep red
5. Sickeningly
6. Emergency medical persons
7. Drenched; soaked
8. The killing of a king
9. Unwilling
10. Energetically
11. Entrust; commit
12. Grieving
13. Bringing to the surface
14. Those who live by preying on others
15. Mean; disgusting
16. Self-satisfied

A=15	B=6	C=9	D=4
E=12	F=1	G=14	H=7
I=2	J=11	K=8	L=13
M=5	N=16	O=3	P=10

Bridge to Terabithia Vocabulary Magic Squares 3

Match the definition with the vocabulary word. Put your answers in the magic squares below. When your answers are correct, all columns and rows will add to the same number.

A. DREAD
B. PANDEMONIUM
C. RELUCTANT
D. PROVERBIAL
E. COMMEND
F. VANQUISHED
G. SPORADICALLY
H. DOUSED
I. CONSPIRING
J. INTOXICATED
K. ACCUSATION
L. DELICATELY
M. OBLIGED
N. PITEOUSLY
O. SPECTACLE
P. GRIT

1. Grateful
2. Defeated
3. Drenched; soaked
4. Public display
5. Sissified manner
6. Unwilling
7. Terror
8. Drunk
9. Guilty charge
10. Obvious
11. Uproar
12. Plotting
13. Pitifully
14. Entrust; commit
15. Occasionally
16. Backbone

A=	B=	C=	D=
E=	F=	G=	H=
I=	J=	K=	L=
M=	N=	O=	P=

Bridge to Terabithia Vocabulary Magic Squares 3 Answer Key

Match the definition with the vocabulary word. Put your answers in the magic squares below. When your answers are correct, all columns and rows will add to the same number.

A. DREAD
B. PANDEMONIUM
C. RELUCTANT
D. PROVERBIAL
E. COMMEND
F. VANQUISHED
G. SPORADICALLY
H. DOUSED
I. CONSPIRING
J. INTOXICATED
K. ACCUSATION
L. DELICATELY
M. OBLIGED
N. PITEOUSLY
O. SPECTACLE
P. GRIT

1. Grateful
2. Defeated
3. Drenched; soaked
4. Public display
5. Sissified manner
6. Unwilling
7. Terror
8. Drunk
9. Guilty charge
10. Obvious
11. Uproar
12. Plotting
13. Pitifully
14. Entrust; commit
15. Occasionally
16. Backbone

A=7	B=11	C=6	D=10
E=14	F=2	G=15	H=3
I=12	J=8	K=9	L=5
M=1	N=13	O=4	P=16

Bridge to Terabithia Vocabulary Magic Squares 4

Match the definition with the vocabulary word. Put your answers in the magic squares below. When your answers are correct, all columns and rows will add to the same number.

A. PANDEMONIUM
B. FOUNDLING
C. CAGEY
D. PARAPETS
E. PUDGY
F. DREDGING
G. VIGOROUSLY
H. CONSOLIDATED
I. REVENGE
J. INCLINED
K. ACCUSATION
L. DESPITE
M. SPECTACLE
N. DELICATELY
O. COMMEND
P. PREDATORS

1. Sissified manner
2. Energetically
3. In spite of
4. Uproar
5. Guilty charge
6. Abandoned infant
7. Public display
8. Conbimed
9. Chubby
10. Those who live by preying on others
11. Tricky; sly
12. Known to; tendency
13. Barriers
14. To get back at; punishment
15. Bringing to the surface
16. Entrust; commit

A=	B=	C=	D=
E=	F=	G=	H=
I=	J=	K=	L=
M=	N=	O=	P=

Bridge to Terabithia Vocabulary Magic Squares 4 Answer Key

Match the definition with the vocabulary word. Put your answers in the magic squares below. When your answers are correct, all columns and rows will add to the same number.

A. PANDEMONIUM   G. VIGOROUSLY   M. SPECTACLE
B. FOUNDLING   H. CONSOLIDATED   N. DELICATELY
C. CAGEY   I. REVENGE   O. COMMEND
D. PARAPETS   J. INCLINED   P. PREDATORS
E. PUDGY   K. ACCUSATION
F. DREDGING   L. DESPITE

1. Sissified manner
2. Energetically
3. In spite of
4. Uproar
5. Guilty charge
6. Abandoned infant
7. Public display
8. Conbimed

9. Chubby
10. Those who live by preying on others
11. Tricky; sly
12. Known to; tendency
13. Barriers
14. To get back at; punishment
15. Bringing to the surface
16. Entrust; commit

A=4	B=6	C=11	D=13
E=9	F=15	G=2	H=8
I=14	J=12	K=5	L=3
M=7	N=1	O=16	P=10

Bridge to Terabithia Vocabulary Word Search 1

```
I N C L I N E D N J V P D Z D Q D F C Y
H O M O D X M E G G E N D I E H Y T J Y
P S O P M S J L Y V O R M F S N H H K K
Z M U U D P N I O I M S E B P C F S M J
G I R D R D L C T P X P V T E J E I U G
D R N G E G L A I B R E V O R P M R I C
O C I Y G A L T C P Q E M C A I E A N P
U W N T S O E E R E R I V X T L E G O L
S D G C S O Q L K E N E C E E M S V M W
E Z E N U X C Y O O G T D N N D T N E P
D T O S Z V E A U B S I T A E G M N D D
W C L L P L I S G T L L C T T E E T N F
R Y D N I I L G E E E I A I L O D V A S
B L E V D Y S P O S Y C G O D N R G P G
G L S X R X A I S R I B S E E E P S H L
J A P L E R K L N X O L Z M D N Q X C Z
T G I W A L Y X O G P U M S H E B A N G
N E T P D T G T L P F O S U R P L U S V
D R E D G I N G C H C D E L D D U M D N
D E T A D I L O S N O C P W Y D L Q V C
```

Backbone (4)
Barriers (8)
Bringing to the surface (8)
Chubby (5)
Comfort (11)
Conbimed (12)
Confused (7)
Deep red (7)
Drenched; soaked (6)
Drunk (11)
Energetically (10)
Entrust; commit (7)
Extra amount (7)
Found; recovered (9)
Glaring; showy (6)
Grateful (7)
Grieving (8)
Hating (9)
Hopeless (9)
In spite of (7)
Known to; tendency (8)
Mean; disgusting (4)
Obvious (10)
Pitifully (9)
Recessed opening (6)
Remains (5)

See; recognize (7)
Self-satisfied (10)
Serious (6)
Sissified manner (10)
Stately; dignified (7)
Terror (5)
The killing of a king (8)
The whole thing (7)
Those who live by preying on others (9)
Threateningly; darkly (9)
To get back at; punishment (7)
Tricky; sly (5)
Uproar (11)
Without stopping (12)

Bridge to Terabithia Vocabulary Word Search 1 Answer Key

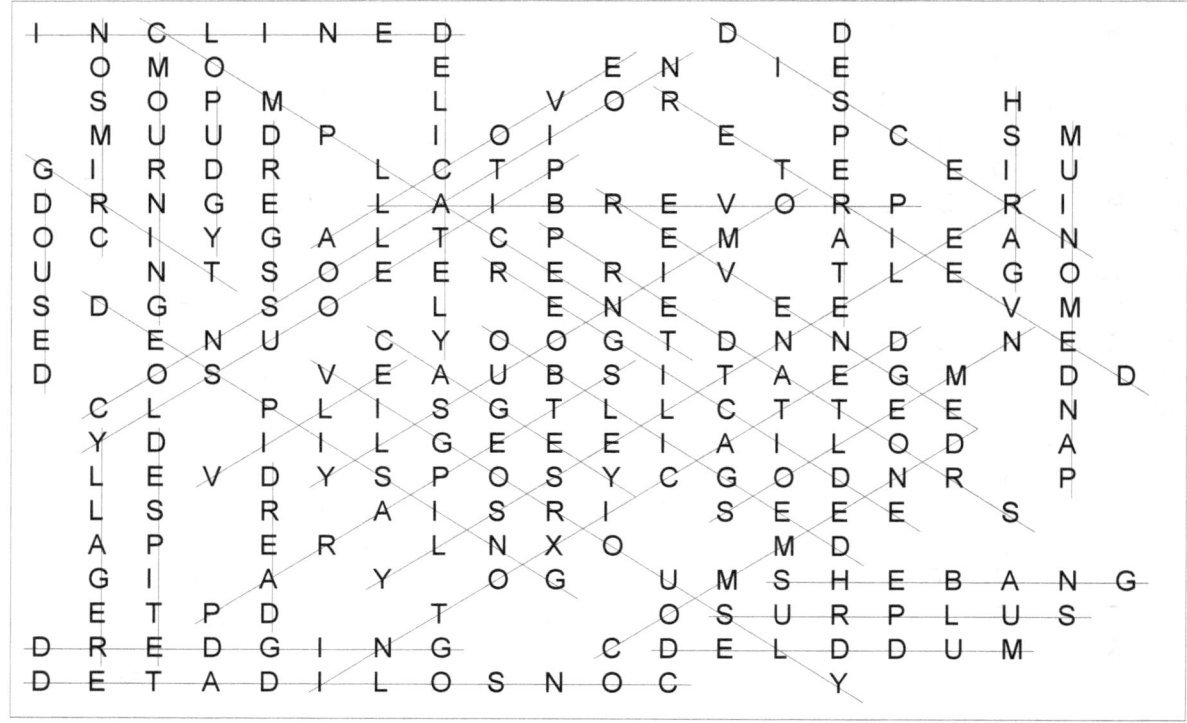

Backbone (4)
Barriers (8)
Bringing to the surface (8)
Chubby (5)
Comfort (11)
Conbimed (12)
Confused (7)
Deep red (7)
Drenched; soaked (6)
Drunk (11)
Energetically (10)
Entrust; commit (7)
Extra amount (7)
Found; recovered (9)
Glaring; showy (6)
Grateful (7)
Grieving (8)
Hating (9)
Hopeless (9)
In spite of (7)
Known to; tendency (8)
Mean; disgusting (4)
Obvious (10)
Pitifully (9)
Recessed opening (6)
Remains (5)

See; recognize (7)
Self-satisfied (10)
Serious (6)
Sissified manner (10)
Stately; dignified (7)
Terror (5)
The killing of a king (8)
The whole thing (7)
Those who live off the prey of others (9)
Threateningly; darkly (9)
To get back at; punishment (7)
Tricky; sly (5)
Uproar (11)
Without stopping (12)

Bridge to Terabithia Vocabulary Word Search 2

```
V Q E G A R I S H S W T D W L R H R N J
X P G T T Y P X C S G N I S I P S E D N
R L N S P T M I R B D X S V K F N T J K
D R E H V T D P R E G I C I D E M R V V
Z R V E Q E G C L J L C E T P B E I I L
B S E B M B G I T Z S E R G P S L E L D
W K R A G F C R I M S O N A L C O V E B
N H R N D A O W O T U I S T T B S E C D
J A Q G T L E U M M N D D U L L Y D B N
P X R E C T K V N R I E D I R E G R I T
R D L E I E X P U D T N G L G P S C C C
P Y E P P R D O R A L E O A E D L S Y F
W A S S S E M R D E D I C U E D G U L N
M E R G P D N I E D S G N N S Y B C S Y
D T E A E E L T N D S C I G G L B N U V
G R F S P O R E E M G L R D Y L Y R O D
D V U Z S E M A K D C I U I Z A R G E Q
W O F N V M T S T N S P N B B G H X T V
D T O H O G H S I E N M F G B E D W I F
M C Y C C O M P L A C E N T C R D Q P H
```

Abandoned infant (9)
Assigned; designated (10)
Backbone (4)
Barriers (8)
Bringing to the surface (8)
Chubby (5)
Conbimed (12)
Confused (7)
Deep red (7)
Drenched; soaked (6)
Emergency medical persons (10)
Entrust; commit (7)
Extra amount (7)
Found; recovered (9)
Glaring; showy (6)
Grateful (7)
Grieving (8)
Hating (9)
Hesitated; wavered (8)
Hopeless (9)
In spite of (7)
Known to; tendency (8)
Mean; disgusting (4)
Pitifully (9)
Recessed opening (6)
Remains (5)

See; recognize (7)
Self-satisfied (10)
Serious (6)
Sissified manner (10)
Stately; dignified (7)
Terror (5)
The killing of a king (8)
The whole thing (7)
Threateningly; darkly (9)
To get back at; punishment (7)
Took back; changed for the better (8)
Tricky; sly (5)
Without stopping (12)

Bridge to Terabithia Vocabulary Word Search 2 Answer Key

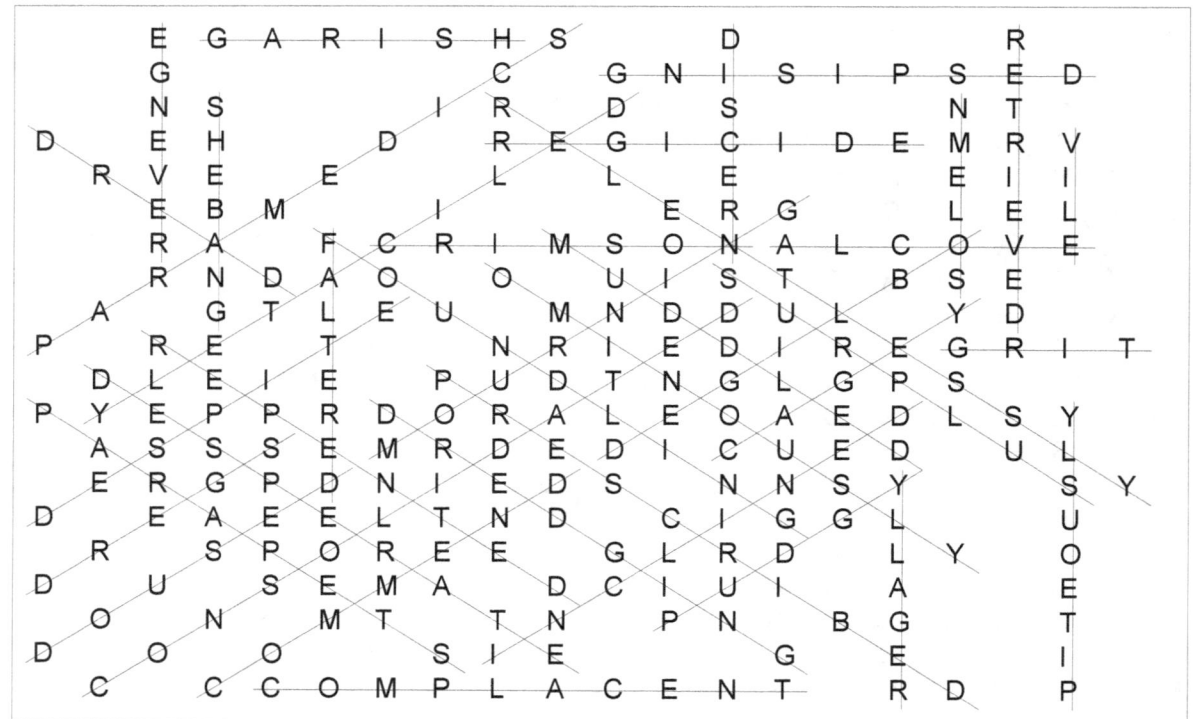

Abandoned infant (9)
Assigned; designated (10)
Backbone (4)
Barriers (8)
Bringing to the surface (8)
Chubby (5)
Conbimed (12)
Confused (7)
Deep red (7)
Drenched; soaked (6)
Emergency medical persons (10)
Entrust; commit (7)
Extra amount (7)
Found; recovered (9)
Glaring; showy (6)
Grateful (7)
Grieving (8)
Hating (9)
Hesitated; wavered (8)
Hopeless (9)
In spite of (7)
Known to; tendency (8)
Mean; disgusting (4)
Pitifully (9)
Recessed opening (6)
Remains (5)

See; recognize (7)
Self-satisfied (10)
Serious (6)
Sissified manner (10)
Stately; dignified (7)
Terror (5)
The killing of a king (8)
The whole thing (7)
Threateningly; darkly (9)
To get back at; punishment (7)
Took back; changed for the better (8)
Tricky; sly (5)
Without stopping (12)

Bridge to Terabithia Vocabulary Word Search 3

```
K Y M D Y P C O N S O L I D A T E D M L
E G N E V E R O R E G I C I D E P G U G
G K S S H G S E D S T S Q A B O N N D B
F F G P T M C Q S C F Y D S G D U I D H
V M C E I R G D X C N E H Z C E Y S L K
H S I R A G A Y R O R E G A L L Y I E H
B C C A Y O G I I E B I Y X S I L P D D
P G B T H D B T T A G T B U P B S S E D
P R Z E U V A L N O D S O E D E S E S B
I I O P G L A G I E R N S N D R E D P D
T C N V U F G N T G I O E N P A L C I P
E Y O C E Q S A Q M E M U S M T T O T C
O M E N L R C U O U M D R S G E N M E B
U P K C S I B G R O I O I N Z L E P G D
S G B S X P N I C P T S I S E Y L L R R
L K L O F M I E A A L G H V C D E A I S
Y T T L V F J R D L D U O E E E R C T F
H N S E Z D F E I E D C S L D C R E G K
I F P M J M R S R N L Q I L T F F N A K
P K M N X P D D P A G V R E P E N T E D
```

ALCOVE	DISCERN	OBLIGED	REVENGE
CAGEY	DOUSED	OMINOUSLY	SHEBANG
COMMEND	DREAD	PITEOUSLY	SOLEMN
COMPLACENT	DREDGING	PREDATORS	SPECULATION
CONSOLIDATED	DREGS	PRESCRIBED	SURPLUS
CONSPIRING	FALTERED	PROVERBIAL	TRAITOROUS
CRIMSON	GARISH	PUDGY	VANQUISHED
DELIBERATELY	GRIT	REGALLY	VILE
DESPERATE	INCLINED	REGICIDE	
DESPISING	INTOXICATED	RELENTLESSLY	
DESPITE	MUDDLED	REPENTED	

Bridge to Terabithia Vocabulary Word Search 3 Answer Key

ALCOVE	DISCERN	OBLIGED	REVENGE
CAGEY	DOUSED	OMINOUSLY	SHEBANG
COMMEND	DREAD	PITEOUSLY	SOLEMN
COMPLACENT	DREDGING	PREDATORS	SPECULATION
CONSOLIDATED	DREGS	PRESCRIBED	SURPLUS
CONSPIRING	FALTERED	PROVERBIAL	TRAITOROUS
CRIMSON	GARISH	PUDGY	VANQUISHED
DELIBERATELY	GRIT	REGALLY	VILE
DESPERATE	INCLINED	REGICIDE	
DESPISING	INTOXICATED	RELENTLESSLY	
DESPITE	MUDDLED	REPENTED	

Bridge to Terabithia Vocabularu Word Search 4

```
R E T R I E V E D E T A D I L O S N O C
R E G I C I D E E S D E S P E R A T E N
F W V B C E M V G O E H P A P Q R X Y K
C A B E S D L M I L T J A N X R D E W T
T R L P N T Q U L E N Y R D L C G X M F
R B I T W G D D B M E R A E V A R O J J
G T S M E W E D O N P T P M C Y U X Q P
E G X J S R T L C R E D E O D R G B S P
C D J D X O E E E O R G T N N R D P L T
O C O M M E N D E G N I S I P S E D W D
M P B W T D A L I I M S N U K C S A P N
P G H W D T I G T S Y G O M U H U G D M
L Q L B O V D C G R C B Y L T M O T P R
A G B R H S I R A G C E A I A L D H D S
C L S G V R E U E C L T R L M T M D H T
E W J G T G T C D D I G D N C H I E C Y
N X D S A C P J S O G G S R W O B O G L
T R N L N F O U N D L I N G E A V D N Y
L O L A I N C L I N E D N X N G U E S L
C Y S P E C T A C L E W R G B P S R C X
```

ALCOVE	DESPITE	INCLINED	REPENTED
CAGEY	DISCERN	MOURNING	RETRIEVED
COMMEND	DOUSED	MUDDLED	REVENGE
COMPLACENT	DREAD	OBLIGED	SANCTUARY
CONSOLATION	DREDGING	PANDEMONIUM	SHEBANG
CONSOLIDATED	DREGS	PARAPETS	SOLEMN
CONSTRICTING	FALTERED	PREDATORS	SPECTACLE
CRIMSON	FOUNDLING	PUDGY	SPECULATION
DESPERATE	GARISH	REGALLY	VILE
DESPISING	GRIT	REGICIDE	

Bridge to Terabithia Vocabulary Word Search 4 Answer Key

```
R E T R I E V E D E T A D I L O S N O C
R E G I C I D E E S D E S P E R A T E Y
F         V       E     G O   E   P A N D       E
C A     E S       M I L E   T   R A D     E
  R L   P N       U D   E M   N   A E   G   M
    I   T M     G D B O N P     P     C   O
    T   M E     E R L C R E     E   M   D R   S
E       S       R O E E E R G T   N   R P
C O M M E N D E G N I S I P S E D
M             A L   I   S N U   C     A
P             T I   T S Y G O M U     S D
L         O V D C     R C     E A L T   U O
A     R H S I R A G     T R I A T   D
C   S       R E U E     D G D N C     I   H   S
E           T G T     D     O   R   O B   G   Y
N         S A C       O G     R E A V D   N
T     N L   F O U N D L I N G   E A V D   N
    O L A I N C L I N E D       N G U E
  C Y S P E C T A C L E         G   P S
```

ALCOVE	DESPITE	INCLINED	REPENTED
CAGEY	DISCERN	MOURNING	RETRIEVED
COMMEND	DOUSED	MUDDLED	REVENGE
COMPLACENT	DREAD	OBLIGED	SANCTUARY
CONSOLATION	DREDGING	PANDEMONIUM	SHEBANG
CONSOLIDATED	DREGS	PARAPETS	SOLEMN
CONSTRICTING	FALTERED	PREDATORS	SPECTACLE
CRIMSON	FOUNDLING	PUDGY	SPECULATION
DESPERATE	GARISH	REGALLY	VILE
DESPISING	GRIT	REGICIDE	

Bridge to Terabithia Vocabulary Crossword 1

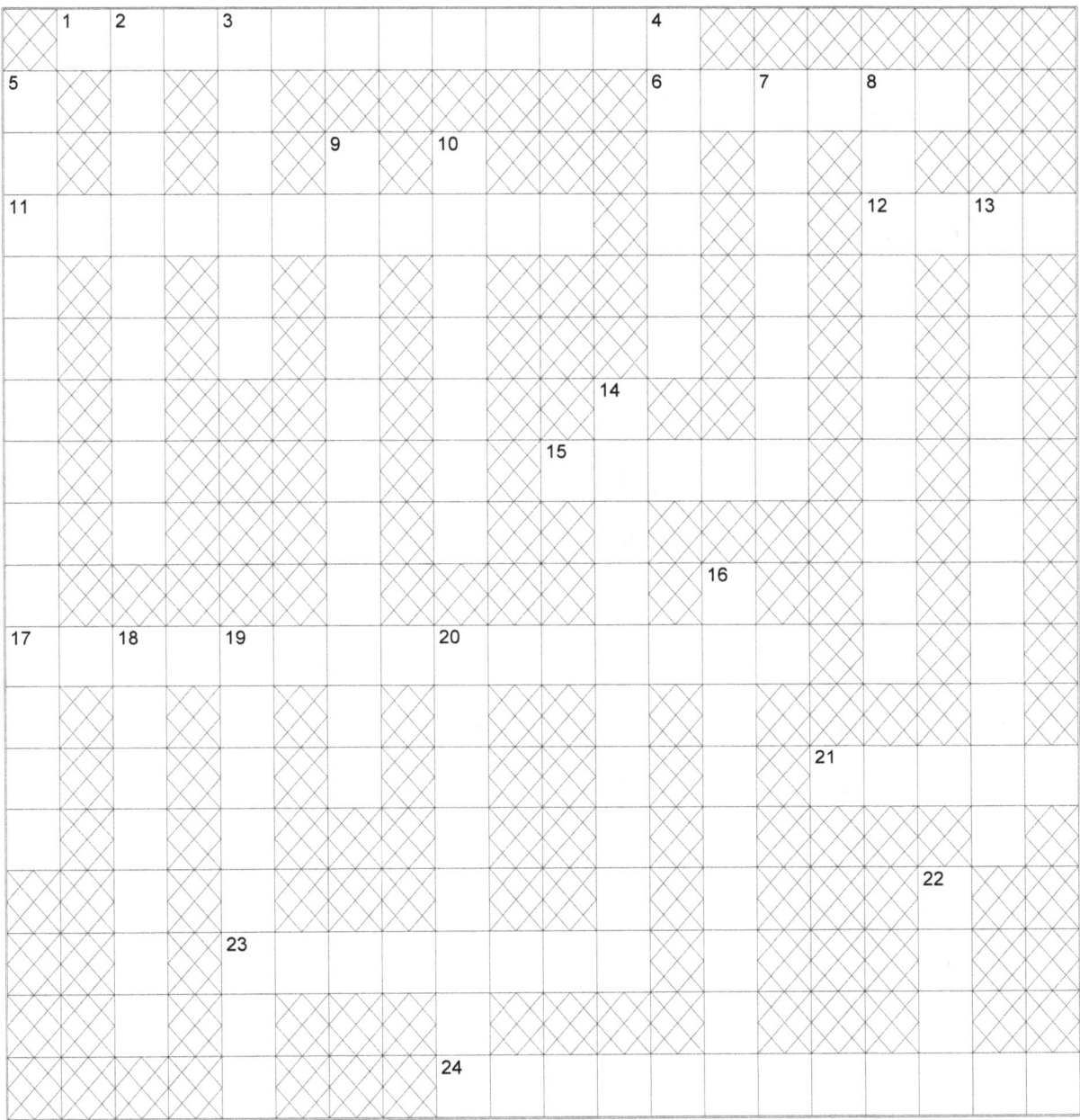

Across
1. Tightening
6. Recessed opening
11. Uproar
12. Backbone
15. Terror
17. Weaknesses
21. Tricky; sly
23. Took back; changed for the better
24. On purpose; intentionally

Down
2. Threateningly; darkly
3. Serious
4. Glaring; showy
5. Two-faced
7. Entrust; commit
8. Energetically
9. Comfort
10. See; recognize
13. Drunk
14. Assigned; designated
16. Hopeless
18. Extra amount
19. Hesitated; wavered
20. Known to; tendency
22. Mean; disgusting

Bridge to Terabithia Vocabulary Crossword 1 Answer Key

Across
1. Tightening
6. Recessed opening
11. Uproar
12. Backbone
15. Terror
17. Weaknesses
21. Tricky; sly
23. Took back; changed for the better
24. On purpose; intentionally

Down
2. Threateningly; darkly
3. Serious
4. Glaring; showy
5. Two-faced
7. Entrust; commit
8. Energetically
9. Comfort
10. See; recognize
13. Drunk
14. Assigned; designated
16. Hopeless
18. Extra amount
19. Hesitated; wavered
20. Known to; tendency
22. Mean; disgusting

Answers (from grid):
- 1 Across: CONSTRICTING
- 6 Across: ALCOVE
- 11 Across: PANDEMONIUM
- 12 Across: GRIT
- 15 Across: DREAD
- 17 Across: INSUFFICIENCIES
- 21 Across: CAGEY
- 23 Across: REPENTED
- 24 Across: DELIBERATELY
- 2 Down: OMINOUSLY
- 3 Down: SOLEMN
- 4 Down: GARISH
- 5 Down: HYPOCRITICAL
- 7 Down: COMMIT
- 8 Down: ENERGETICALLY (EMMESHLY... see grid)
- 9 Down: CONSOLATION
- 10 Down: DISCERN
- 13 Down: INTOXICATED
- 14 Down: PREDESTINED
- 16 Down: DESPAIRINGLY
- 18 Down: SURPLUS
- 19 Down: FALTERED
- 20 Down: INCLINED
- 22 Down: VILE

Bridge to Terabithia Vocabulary Crossword 2

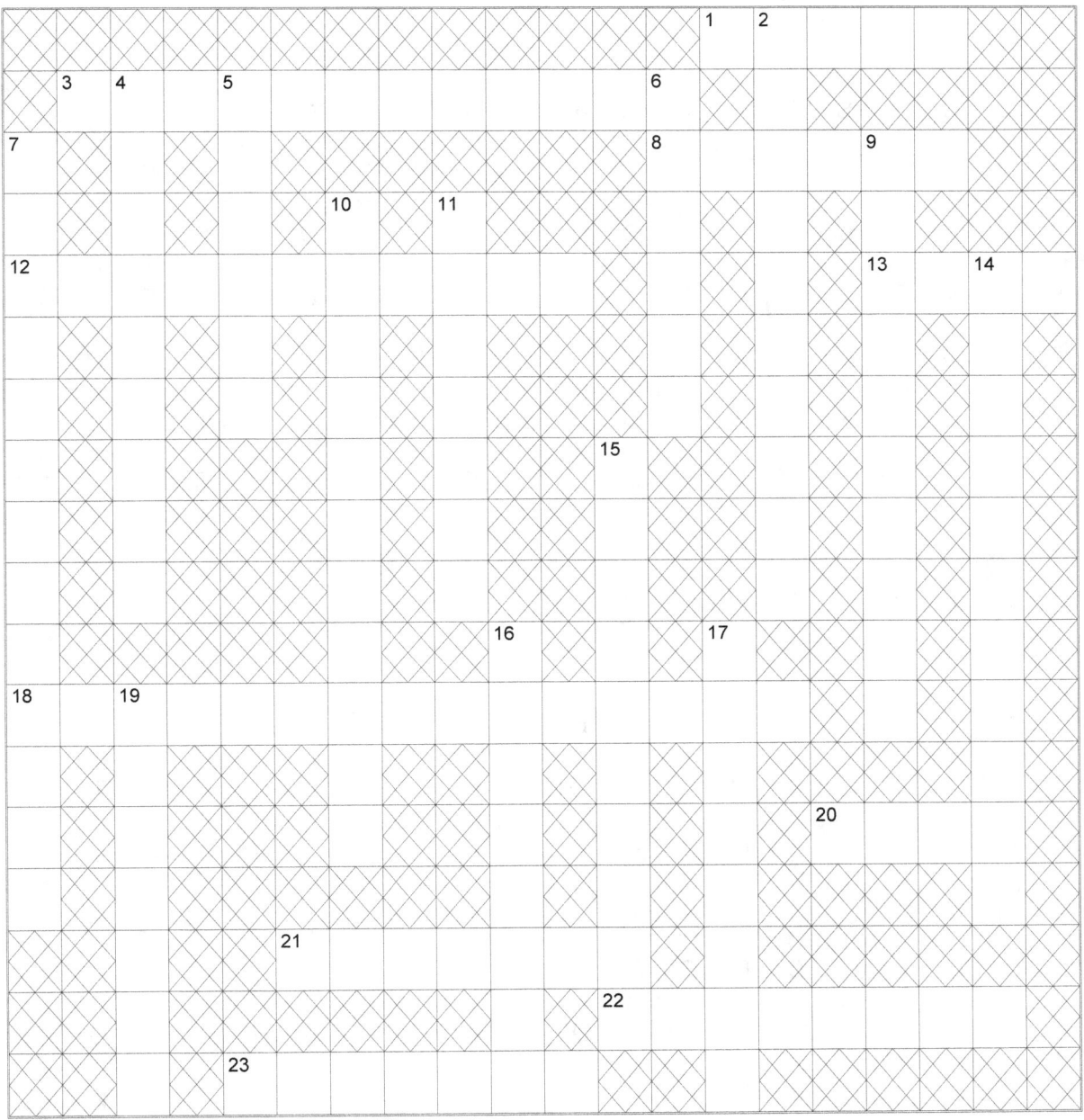

Across
1. Tricky; sly
3. Tightening
8. Recessed opening
12. Uproar
13. Backbone
18. Weaknesses
20. Mean; disgusting
21. In spite of
22. Bringing to the surface
23. Grateful

Down
2. Guilty charge
4. Threateningly; darkly
5. Serious
6. Glaring; showy
7. Two-faced
9. Energetically
10. Comfort
11. See; recognize
14. Drunk
15. Assigned; designated
16. The killing of a king
17. Took back; changed for the better
19. Extra amount

Bridge to Terabithia Vocabulary Crossword 2 Answer Key

```
                              C A G E Y
        C O N S T R I C T I N G   C
      H   M   O               A L C O V E
      Y   I   L   C   D       R   U   G   T
      P A N D E M O N I U M   I   S   G R I T
      O   O   M   N   S       S   A   O   N
      C   U   N   S   C       H   T   R   T
      R   S       O   E     P     I   O   O
      I   L       L   R     R     O   U   X
      I   Y       A   N     E     N   S   I
      T           T   R S   R     L   C
      I N S U F F I C I E N C I E S   Y   A
      C   U       O   G   R   P           T
      A   R       N   I   I   E   V I L E
      L   P       N   C   B   N           D
              D E S P I T E   T
                      D   D R E D G I N G
              S O B L I G E D   D
```

Across
1. Tricky; sly
3. Tightening
8. Recessed opening
12. Uproar
13. Backbone
18. Weaknesses
20. Mean; disgusting
21. In spite of
22. Bringing to the surface
23. Grateful

Down
2. Guilty charge
4. Threateningly; darkly
5. Serious
6. Glaring; showy
7. Two-faced
9. Energetically
10. Comfort
11. See; recognize
14. Drunk
15. Assigned; designated
16. The killing of a king
17. Took back; changed for the better
19. Extra amount

Bridge to Terabithia Vocabulary Crossword 3

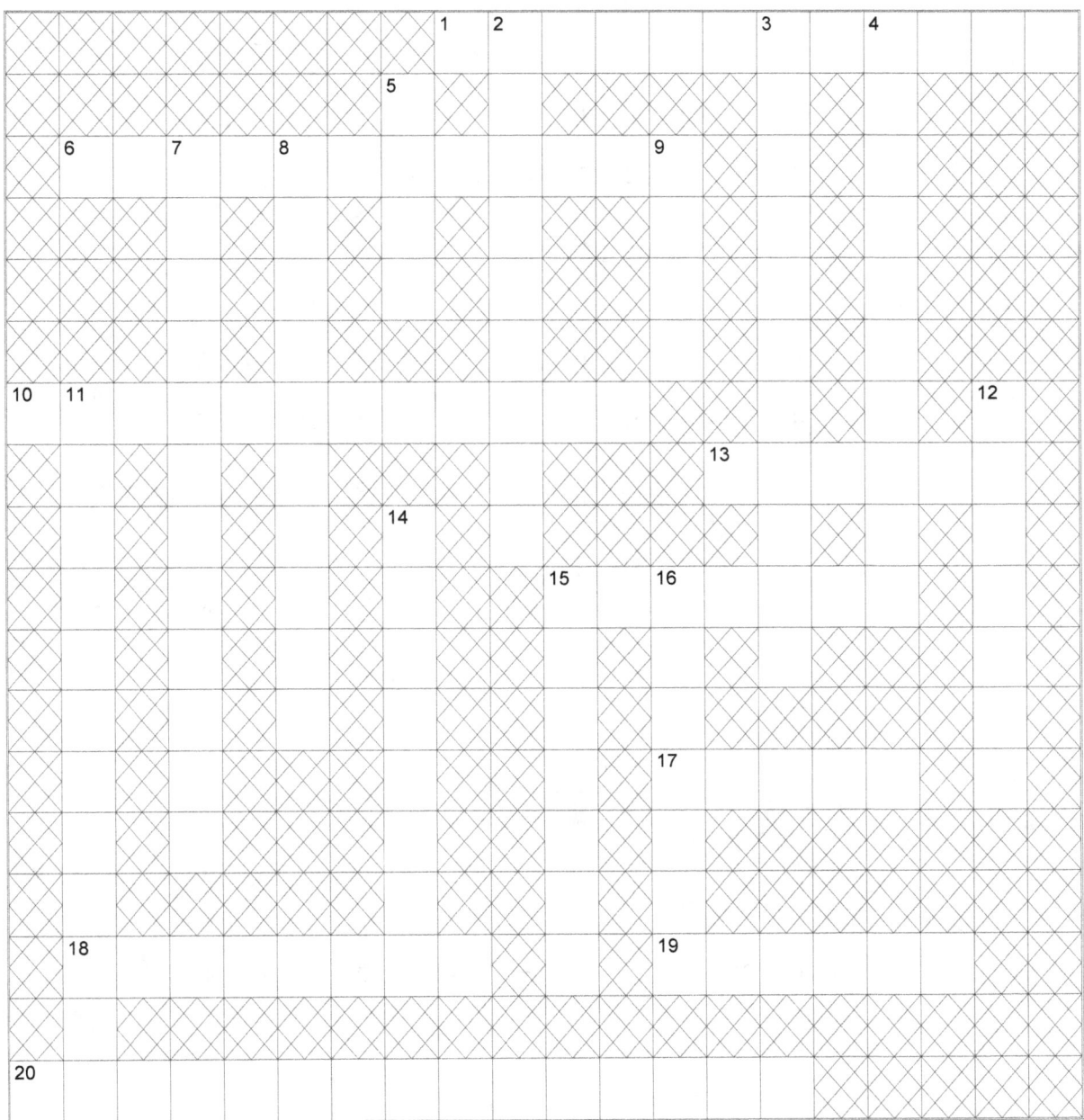

Across
1. Occasionally
6. Tightening
10. Without stopping
13. Glaring; showy
15. See; recognize
17. Chubby
18. Known to; tendency
19. Serious
20. Weaknesses

Down
2. Pitifully
3. Drunk
4. Guilty charge
5. Mean; disgusting
7. Sickeningly
8. Disloyal; back-stabbing
9. Backbone
11. Thrill
12. The whole thing
14. The killing of a king
15. In spite of
16. Extra amount

Bridge to Terabithia Vocabulary Crossword 3 Answer Key

Across
1. Occasionally
6. Tightening
10. Without stopping
13. Glaring; showy
15. See; recognize
17. Chubby
18. Known to; tendency
19. Serious
20. Weaknesses

Down
2. Pitifully
3. Drunk
4. Guilty charge
5. Mean; disgusting
7. Sickeningly
8. Disloyal; back-stabbing
9. Backbone
11. Thrill
12. The whole thing
14. The killing of a king
15. In spite of
16. Extra amount

Bridge to Terabithia Vocabulary Crosswrod 4

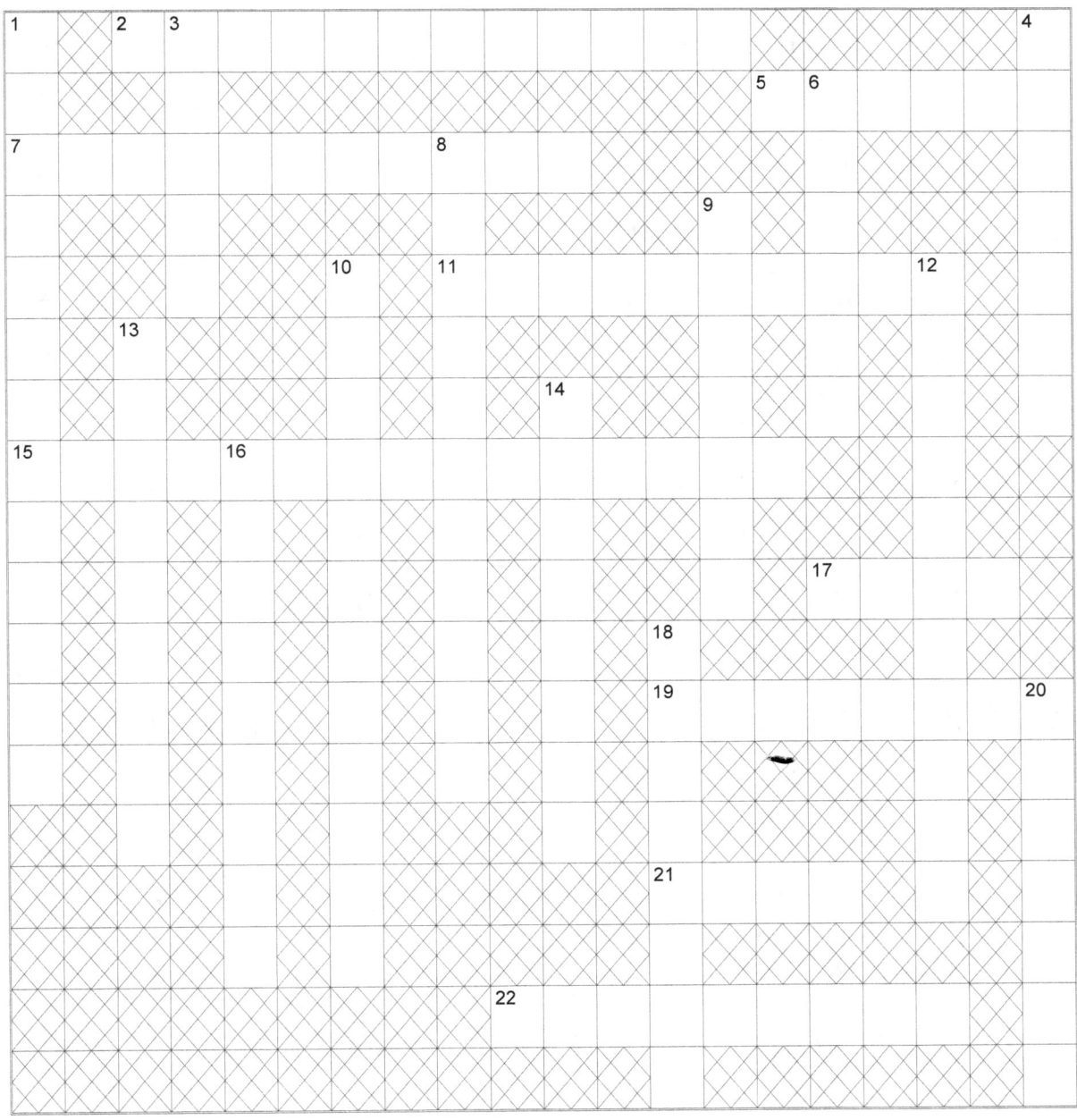

Across
2. Occasionally
5. Glaring; showy
7. Uproar
11. Disloyal; back-stabbing
15. Weaknesses
17. Mean; disgusting
19. Took back; changed for the better
21. Backbone
22. Threateningly; darkly

Down
1. Two-faced
3. Chubby
4. The whole thing
6. Recessed opening
8. Drunk
9. Entrust; commit
10. Thrill
12. Consideration; thought
13. Hopeless
14. Known to; tendency
16. Abandoned infant
18. Bringing to the surface
20. In spite of

Bridge to Terabithia Vocabulary Crossword 4 Answer Key

Across
2. Occasionally
5. Glaring; showy
7. Uproar
11. Disloyal; back-stabbing
15. Weaknesses
17. Mean; disgusting
19. Took back; changed for the better
21. Backbone
22. Threateningly; darkly

Down
1. Two-faced
3. Chubby
4. The whole thing
6. Recessed opening
8. Drunk
9. Entrust; commit
10. Thrill
12. Consideration; thought
13. Hopeless
14. Known to; tendency
16. Abandoned infant
18. Bringing to the surface
20. In spite of

Bridge to Terabithia Vocabulary Juggle Letters 1

1. RDADE = 1. _____
   Terror

2. MOECDMN = 2. _____
   Entrust; commit

3. UGDYP = 3. _____
   Chubby

4. SYTIEOLPU = 4. _____
   Pitifully

5. ICDERSN = 5. _____
   See; recognize

6. RSGDE = 6. _____
   Remains

7. TNCSCNIGORTI = 7. _____
   Tightening

8. ANSRYACTU = 8. _____
   Place of worship

9. RAROBPVLIE = 9. _____
   Obvious

10. ITGR =10. _____
    Backbone

11. EDNGDGIR =11. _____
    Bringing to the surface

12. POYRAADLISLC =12. _____
    Occasionally

13. ELCMTAPCON =13. _____
    Self-satisfied

14. UIGMNRON =14. _____
    Grieving

15. OUMYLIONS =15. _____
    Threateningly; darkly

Bridge to Terabithia Vocabulary Jugle Letters 1 Answer Key

1. RDADE = 1. DREAD
Terror

2. MOECDMN = 2. COMMEND
Entrust; commit

3. UGDYP = 3. PUDGY
Chubby

4. SYTIEOLPU = 4. PITEOUSLY
Pitifully

5. ICDERSN = 5. DISCERN
See; recognize

6. RSGDE = 6. DREGS
Remains

7. TNCSCNIGORTI = 7. CONSTRICTING
Tightening

8. ANSRYACTU = 8. SANCTUARY
Place of worship

9. RAROBPVLIE = 9. PROVERBIAL
Obvious

10. ITGR = 10. GRIT
Backbone

11. EDNGDGIR = 11. DREDGING
Bringing to the surface

12. POYRAADLISLC = 12. SPORADICALLY
Occasionally

13. ELCMTAPCON = 13. COMPLACENT
Self-satisfied

14. UIGMNRON = 14. MOURNING
Grieving

15. OUMYLIONS = 15. OMINOUSLY
Threateningly; darkly

Bridge to Terabithia Vocabulary Juggle Letters 2

1. OIXTCDENAIT = 1. _____
   Drunk

2. MPOIDENUAMN = 2. _____
   Uproar

3. SEIERRBCDP = 3. _____
   Assigned; designated

4. NEITGSNUAYAL = 4. _____
   Sickeningly

5. RATXENHAOIIL = 5. _____
   Thrill

6. TCOSAAINCU = 6. _____
   Guilty charge

7. ESRDG = 7. _____
   Remains

8. GEBDLOI = 8. _____
   Grateful

9. URSSPLU = 9. _____
   Extra amount

10. RUIGNMNO = 10. _____
    Grieving

11. EDNRGIDG = 11. _____
    Bringing to the surface

12. ADERD = 12. _____
    Terror

13. SEPRDAIAMC = 13. _____
    Emergency medical persons

14. VRIAPROELB = 14. _____
    Obvious

15. ESRTODPAR = 15. _____
    Those who live by preying on others

Bridge to Terabithia Vocabulary Juggle Letters 2 Answer Key

1. OIXTCDENAIT = 1. INTOXICATED
   Drunk
2. MPOIDENUAMN = 2. PANDEMONIUM
   Uproar
3. SEIERRBCDP = 3. PRESCRIBED
   Assigned; designated
4. NEITGSNUAYAL = 4. NAUSEATINGLY
   Sickeningly
5. RATXENHAOIIL = 5. EXHILARATION
   Thrill
6. TCOSAAINCU = 6. ACCUSATION
   Guilty charge
7. ESRDG = 7. DREGS
   Remains
8. GEBDLOI = 8. OBLIGED
   Grateful
9. URSSPLU = 9. SURPLUS
   Extra amount
10. RUIGNMNO =10. MOURNING
    Grieving
11. EDNRGIDG =11. DREDGING
    Bringing to the surface
12. ADERD =12. DREAD
    Terror
13. SEPRDAIAMC =13. PARAMEDICS
    Emergency medical persons
14. VRIAPROELB =14. PROVERBIAL
    Obvious
15. ESRTODPAR =15. PREDATORS
    Those who live by preying on others

Bridge to Terabithia Vocabulary Juggle Letters 3

1. NACEPTOCLM = 1. _____
   Self-satisfied

2. GONMIUNR = 2. _____
   Grieving

3. REAIBLEDELYT = 3. _____
   On purpose; intentionally

4. SRPBCRDIEE = 4. _____
   Assigned; designated

5. ETILOPUYS = 5. _____
   Pitifully

6. CLTYHIAROIPIC = 6. _____
   Two-faced

7. LAEAYUTSNIGN = 7. _____
   Sickeningly

8. DDEOUS = 8. _____
   Drenched; soaked

9. DDETISOOCALN = 9. _____
   Conbimed

10. ENLSTIOCAUP =10. _____
    Consideration; thought

11. DMONIAEPMNU =11. _____
    Uproar

12. MREAICADPS =12. _____
    Emergency medical persons

13. IDSETPE =13. _____
    In spite of

14. CSALRDAIYLOP =14. _____
    Occasionally

15. LLYAREG =15. _____
    Stately; dignified

Bridge to Terabithia Vocabulary Juggle Letters 3 Answer Key

1. NACEPTOCLM = 1. COMPLACENT
   Self-satisfied

2. GONMIUNR = 2. MOURNING
   Grieving

3. REAIBLEDELYT = 3. DELIBERATELY
   On purpose; intentionally

4. SRPBCRDIEE = 4. PRESCRIBED
   Assigned; designated

5. ETILOPUYS = 5. PITEOUSLY
   Pitifully

6. CLTYHIAROIPIC = 6. HYPOCRIITICAL
   Two-faced

7. LAEAYUTSNIGN = 7. NAUSEATINGLY
   Sickeningly

8. DDEOUS = 8. DOUSED
   Drenched; soaked

9. DDETISOOCALN = 9. CONSOLIDATED
   Conbimed

10. ENLSTIOCAUP = 10. SPECULATION
    Consideration; thought

11. DMONIAEPMNU = 11. PANDEMONIUM
    Uproar

12. MREAICADPS = 12. PARAMEDICS
    Emergency medical persons

13. IDSETPE = 13. DESPITE
    In spite of

14. CSALRDAIYLOP = 14. SPORADICALLY
    Occasionally

15. LLYAREG = 15. REGALLY
    Stately; dignified

Bridge to Terabithia Vocabulary Juggle Letters 4

1. DMDUDLE = 1. _____
   Confused

2. ANSOTOLOCIN = 2. _____
   Comfort

3. EUTPLSYOI = 3. _____
   Pitifully

4. TCEPOMCNLA = 4. _____
   Self-satisfied

5. ADRDE = 5. _____
   Terror

6. DGIDRNGE = 6. _____
   Bringing to the surface

7. DNLNUGOFI = 7. _____
   Abandoned infant

8. AUITRRTSOO = 8. _____
   Disloyal; back-stabbing

9. EVRIDERTE = 9. _____
   Found; recovered

10. TECCEASPL =10. _____
    Public display

11. HISRAG =11. _____
    Glaring; showy

12. EDMANUMIPON =12. _____
    Uproar

13. ESRTLESLLENY =13. _____
    Without stopping

14. ESDUOD =14. _____
    Drenched; soaked

15. PTDREENE =15. _____
    Took back; changed for the better

Bridge to Terabithia Vocabulary Juggle Letters 4 Answer Key

1. DMDUDLE = 1. MUDDLED
Confused

2. ANSOTOLOCIN = 2. CONSOLATION
Comfort

3. EUTPLSYOI = 3. PITEOUSLY
Pitifully

4. TCEPOMCNLA = 4. COMPLACENT
Self-satisfied

5. ADRDE = 5. DREAD
Terror

6. DGIDRNGE = 6. DREDGING
Bringing to the surface

7. DNLNUGOFI = 7. FOUNDLING
Abandoned infant

8. AUITRRTSOO = 8. TRAITOROUS
Disloyal; back-stabbing

9. EVRIDERTE = 9. RETRIEVED
Found; recovered

10. TECCEASPL = 10. SPECTACLE
Public display

11. HISRAG = 11. GARISH
Glaring; showy

12. EDMANUMIPON = 12. PANDEMONIUM
Uproar

13. ESRTLESLLENY = 13. RELENTLESSLY
Without stopping

14. ESDUOD = 14. DOUSED
Drenched; soaked

15. PTDREENE = 15. REPENTED
Took back; changed for the better

ACCUSATION	Guilty charge
ALCOVE	Recessed opening
CAGEY	Tricky; sly
COMMEND	Entrust; commit
COMPLACENT	Self-satisfied
CONSOLATION	Comfort

CONSOLIDATED	Conbimed
CONSPIRING	Plotting
CONSTRICTING	Tightening
CRIMSON	Deep red
DELIBERATELY	On purpose; intentionally
DELICATELY	Sissified manner

DESPERATE	Hopeless
DESPISING	Hating
DESPITE	In spite of
DISCERN	See; recognize
DOUSED	Drenched; soaked
DREAD	Terror

DREDGING	Bringing to the surface
DREGS	Remains
EXHILARATION	Thrill
FALTERED	Hesitated; wavered
FOUNDLING	Abandoned infant
GARISH	Glaring; showy

GRIT	Backbone
HYPOCRIITICAL	Two-faced
INCLINED	Known to; tendency
INSUFFICIENCIES	Weaknesses
INTOXICATED	Drunk
MOURNING	Grieving

MUDDLED	Confused
NAUSEATINGLY	Sickeningly
OBLIGED	Grateful
OMINOUSLY	Threateningly; darkly
PANDEMONIUM	Uproar
PARAMEDICS	Emergency medical persons

PARAPETS	Barriers
PITEOUSLY	Pitifully
PREDATORS	Those who live by preying on others
PRESCRIBED	Assigned; designated
PROVERBIAL	Obvious
PUDGY	Chubby

REGALLY	Stately; dignified
REGICIDE	The killing of a king
RELENTLESSLY	Without stopping
RELUCTANT	Unwilling
REPENTED	Took back; changed for the better
RETRIEVED	Found; recovered

REVENGE	To get back at; punishment
SANCTUARY	Place of worship
SHEBANG	The whole thing
SOLEMN	Serious
SPECTACLE	Public display
SPECULATION	Consideration; thought

SPORADICALLY	Occasionally
SURPLUS	Extra amount
TRAITOROUS	Disloyal; back-stabbing
VANQUISHED	Defeated
VIGOROUSLY	Energetically
VILE	Mean; disgusting

Bridge to Terabithia Vocabulary

DOUSED	PUDGY	SOLEMN	PARAPETS	SANCTUARY
DREDGING	TRAITOROUS	FALTERED	DREGS	CAGEY
GARISH	SPECULATION	FREE SPACE	INTOXICATED	PITEOUSLY
DESPERATE	MUDDLED	EXHILARATION	COMPLACENT	RELENTLESSLY
DREAD	DISCERN	RELUCTANT	CONSOLATION	CONSOLIDATED

Bridge to Terabithia Vocabulary

DESPITE	CRIMSON	ACCUSATION	CONSTRICTING	VILE
PROVERBIAL	REGICIDE	PREDATORS	COMMEND	INSUFFICIENCIES
REVENGE	PARAMEDICS	FREE SPACE	DESPISING	VIGOROUSLY
DELICATELY	OMINOUSLY	FOUNDLING	DELIBERATELY	SPECTACLE
SHEBANG	PANDEMONIUM	NAUSEATINGLY	REGALLY	ALCOVE

Bridge to Terabithia Vocabulary

PARAPETS	MUDDLED	NAUSEATINGLY	SHEBANG	PITEOUSLY
SPECTACLE	DREGS	SPORADICALLY	PUDGY	TRAITOROUS
COMPLACENT	DELICATELY	FREE SPACE	VANQUISHED	REGALLY
DOUSED	FOUNDLING	CONSOLATION	DREDGING	OBLIGED
CONSOLIDATED	GRIT	INTOXICATED	DESPITE	CAGEY

Bridge to Terabithia Vocabulary

CRIMSON	SURPLUS	SANCTUARY	ALCOVE	PREDATORS
RETRIEVED	CONSTRICTING	REPENTED	COMMEND	VIGOROUSLY
RELUCTANT	MOURNING	FREE SPACE	GARISH	DESPERATE
OMINOUSLY	DREAD	DISCERN	HYPOCRIITICAL	REVENGE
REGICIDE	FALTERED	PROVERBIAL	SPECULATION	INCLINED

Bridge to Terabithia Vocabulary

ALCOVE	PARAMEDICS	DESPISING	PARAPETS	SOLEMN
OBLIGED	REGALLY	SURPLUS	OMINOUSLY	INTOXICATED
CONSOLIDATED	RELENTLESSLY	FREE SPACE	FOUNDLING	CONSPIRING
SPECTACLE	HYPOCRIITICAL	DREDGING	DESPERATE	VIGOROUSLY
SHEBANG	PRESCRIBED	INSUFFICIENCIES	DOUSED	SPORADICALLY

Bridge to Terabithia Vocabulary

COMMEND	RETRIEVED	CONSOLATION	PREDATORS	GARISH
REPENTED	PANDEMONIUM	REVENGE	CRIMSON	GRIT
RELUCTANT	MUDDLED	FREE SPACE	PITEOUSLY	VILE
REGICIDE	MOURNING	ACCUSATION	DREAD	FALTERED
SANCTUARY	COMPLACENT	NAUSEATINGLY	DELIBERATELY	INCLINED

Bridge to Terabithia Vocabulary

DESPERATE	VIGOROUSLY	PARAPETS	REGALLY	PITEOUSLY
ALCOVE	DOUSED	PROVERBIAL	OBLIGED	DESPISING
DESPITE	CONSOLIDATED	FREE SPACE	COMPLACENT	GARISH
DELICATELY	CAGEY	RETRIEVED	REPENTED	SHEBANG
RELUCTANT	DREGS	TRAITOROUS	SURPLUS	INCLINED

Bridge to Terabithia Vocabulary

CRIMSON	PARAMEDICS	SOLEMN	FALTERED	GRIT
ACCUSATION	PRESCRIBED	INTOXICATED	SPECULATION	SANCTUARY
REVENGE	DELIBERATELY	FREE SPACE	NAUSEATINGLY	RELENTLESSLY
CONSOLATION	VANQUISHED	PANDEMONIUM	PREDATORS	EXHILARATION
REGICIDE	DISCERN	FOUNDLING	DREAD	MUDDLED

Bridge to Terabithia Vocabulary

CONSOLIDATED	CONSPIRING	NAUSEATINGLY	SPORADICALLY	VIGOROUSLY
VANQUISHED	EXHILARATION	FALTERED	DREAD	FOUNDLING
PANDEMONIUM	SPECTACLE	FREE SPACE	PRESCRIBED	DELICATELY
PUDGY	GRIT	PREDATORS	GARISH	REPENTED
PROVERBIAL	INCLINED	RETRIEVED	REGICIDE	REGALLY

Bridge to Terabithia Vocabulary

DESPERATE	DELIBERATELY	MOURNING	RELENTLESSLY	VILE
TRAITOROUS	HYPOCRIITICAL	DREDGING	SURPLUS	COMPLACENT
CRIMSON	DREGS	FREE SPACE	DESPITE	CAGEY
SHEBANG	COMMEND	DESPISING	ACCUSATION	REVENGE
INSUFFICIENCIES	DISCERN	PARAPETS	PARAMEDICS	OMINOUSLY

Bridge to Terabithia Vocabulary

FOUNDLING	PARAPETS	MOURNING	ACCUSATION	PREDATORS
OMINOUSLY	SURPLUS	PANDEMONIUM	COMMEND	DREDGING
DREGS	GARISH	FREE SPACE	DESPITE	SANCTUARY
REGICIDE	PROVERBIAL	RELUCTANT	ALCOVE	REPENTED
SHEBANG	SOLEMN	DESPERATE	SPECTACLE	FALTERED

Bridge to Terabithia Vocabulary

NAUSEATINGLY	CONSTRICTING	INCLINED	CAGEY	PUDGY
CRIMSON	OBLIGED	MUDDLED	DISCERN	VILE
CONSOLATION	HYPOCRIITICAL	FREE SPACE	GRIT	RELENTLESSLY
PARAMEDICS	DESPISING	DELIBERATELY	PRESCRIBED	VIGOROUSLY
INSUFFICIENCIES	REVENGE	COMPLACENT	CONSPIRING	DOUSED

Bridge to Terabithia Vocabulary

INSUFFICIENCIES	GRIT	DESPERATE	DESPISING	FALTERED
PROVERBIAL	RELUCTANT	OBLIGED	DREDGING	SPECULATION
COMMEND	SPORADICALLY	FREE SPACE	RETRIEVED	DREAD
CONSTRICTING	REGICIDE	INTOXICATED	REGALLY	DOUSED
GARISH	PITEOUSLY	REPENTED	PREDATORS	SOLEMN

Bridge to Terabithia Vocabulary

CONSPIRING	PRESCRIBED	RELENTLESSLY	INCLINED	DESPITE
REVENGE	PANDEMONIUM	DREGS	OMINOUSLY	COMPLACENT
MUDDLED	DELICATELY	FREE SPACE	ACCUSATION	HYPOCRIITICAL
FOUNDLING	SANCTUARY	CRIMSON	DELIBERATELY	SPECTACLE
TRAITOROUS	PARAPETS	VILE	VANQUISHED	CAGEY

Bridge to Terabithia Vocabulary

OBLIGED	RELENTLESSLY	SANCTUARY	ACCUSATION	VANQUISHED
CONSOLATION	SOLEMN	PRESCRIBED	PREDATORS	DESPITE
DREGS	OMINOUSLY	FREE SPACE	CRIMSON	DREAD
MOURNING	TRAITOROUS	VIGOROUSLY	DISCERN	REGALLY
NAUSEATINGLY	SHEBANG	CAGEY	RELUCTANT	DREDGING

Bridge to Terabithia Vocabulary

PITEOUSLY	REVENGE	DELIBERATELY	INTOXICATED	SPECTACLE
HYPOCRIITICAL	CONSTRICTING	FALTERED	VILE	PUDGY
CONSPIRING	PANDEMONIUM	FREE SPACE	EXHILARATION	COMMEND
SPECULATION	DELICATELY	REPENTED	PARAPETS	SURPLUS
DESPERATE	REGICIDE	RETRIEVED	PROVERBIAL	SPORADICALLY

Bridge to Terabithia Vocabulary

FOUNDLING	RELENTLESSLY	MOURNING	DISCERN	CAGEY
FALTERED	OMINOUSLY	DREDGING	RELUCTANT	REGALLY
INTOXICATED	RETRIEVED	FREE SPACE	REPENTED	CONSTRICTING
VILE	DESPISING	SPECULATION	OBLIGED	ACCUSATION
CONSOLATION	SPORADICALLY	PREDATORS	SHEBANG	SOLEMN

Bridge to Terabithia Vocabulary

NAUSEATINGLY	COMPLACENT	COMMEND	PRESCRIBED	VIGOROUSLY
GRIT	PARAMEDICS	DELIBERATELY	VANQUISHED	INSUFFICIENCIES
DESPERATE	DREGS	FREE SPACE	INCLINED	EXHILARATION
REVENGE	SANCTUARY	DELICATELY	HYPOCRIITICAL	PROVERBIAL
DESPITE	SURPLUS	CONSPIRING	TRAITOROUS	PARAPETS

Bridge to Terabithia Vocabulary

GARISH	PROVERBIAL	PREDATORS	INTOXICATED	TRAITOROUS
EXHILARATION	RELUCTANT	REGALLY	PARAPETS	VILE
VANQUISHED	VIGOROUSLY	FREE SPACE	ACCUSATION	CONSOLATION
COMMEND	DESPERATE	CONSTRICTING	COMPLACENT	RELENTLESSLY
SOLEMN	DESPITE	CONSOLIDATED	SURPLUS	PITEOUSLY

Bridge to Terabithia Vocabulary

REGICIDE	DISCERN	DREAD	DELIBERATELY	DELICATELY
DESPISING	OMINOUSLY	FOUNDLING	PUDGY	SPORADICALLY
PANDEMONIUM	OBLIGED	FREE SPACE	SPECTACLE	REPENTED
ALCOVE	GRIT	INCLINED	MUDDLED	NAUSEATINGLY
HYPOCRIITICAL	DREDGING	INSUFFICIENCIES	SPECULATION	MOURNING

Bridge to Terabithia Vocabulary

PARAMEDICS	DOUSED	RELUCTANT	COMPLACENT	REVENGE
CAGEY	INSUFFICIENCIES	COMMEND	CONSTRICTING	DESPISING
VANQUISHED	PUDGY	FREE SPACE	CONSOLIDATED	INTOXICATED
NAUSEATINGLY	PARAPETS	RETRIEVED	PRESCRIBED	VILE
INCLINED	DREDGING	REPENTED	DISCERN	FALTERED

Bridge to Terabithia Vocabulary

OBLIGED	ALCOVE	MUDDLED	PANDEMONIUM	REGALLY
PITEOUSLY	RELENTLESSLY	SOLEMN	SURPLUS	SPECULATION
PROVERBIAL	SHEBANG	FREE SPACE	SPECTACLE	CONSOLATION
DREAD	CRIMSON	ACCUSATION	EXHILARATION	CONSPIRING
DREGS	REGICIDE	MOURNING	FOUNDLING	OMINOUSLY

Bridge to Terabithia Vocabulary

VANQUISHED	OBLIGED	MOURNING	VILE	FALTERED
INSUFFICIENCIES	DREGS	CAGEY	FOUNDLING	GARISH
PANDEMONIUM	OMINOUSLY	FREE SPACE	PITEOUSLY	SOLEMN
DELIBERATELY	RELUCTANT	HYPOCRIITICAL	CRIMSON	DREAD
DESPISING	CONSOLIDATED	COMPLACENT	DREDGING	DESPITE

Bridge to Terabithia Vocabulary

ALCOVE	SPECULATION	INCLINED	CONSPIRING	REPENTED
PRESCRIBED	GRIT	MUDDLED	REGALLY	CONSTRICTING
SPORADICALLY	DELICATELY	FREE SPACE	DESPERATE	PARAMEDICS
CONSOLATION	PREDATORS	NAUSEATINGLY	SURPLUS	SHEBANG
ACCUSATION	INTOXICATED	PUDGY	SANCTUARY	EXHILARATION

Bridge to Terabithia Vocabulary

DREGS	MOURNING	NAUSEATINGLY	INCLINED	REGICIDE
SANCTUARY	RELUCTANT	CONSPIRING	PROVERBIAL	DESPITE
PREDATORS	VIGOROUSLY	FREE SPACE	DOUSED	CONSOLATION
VILE	PRESCRIBED	DESPERATE	ALCOVE	RETRIEVED
PARAMEDICS	CONSTRICTING	CRIMSON	PITEOUSLY	SURPLUS

Bridge to Terabithia Vocabulary

REGALLY	SPORADICALLY	DREAD	DISCERN	EXHILARATION
REVENGE	INSUFFICIENCIES	COMMEND	OBLIGED	HYPOCRIITICAL
CAGEY	VANQUISHED	FREE SPACE	RELENTLESSLY	DREDGING
PARAPETS	ACCUSATION	SPECULATION	FOUNDLING	INTOXICATED
SPECTACLE	PUDGY	TRAITOROUS	CONSOLIDATED	FALTERED

Bridge to Terabithia Vocabulary

SURPLUS	INTOXICATED	CRIMSON	DESPITE	NAUSEATINGLY
GRIT	DREAD	RELUCTANT	SPECTACLE	PARAMEDICS
RETRIEVED	EXHILARATION	FREE SPACE	VILE	GARISH
ALCOVE	CONSOLATION	REGALLY	REGICIDE	OMINOUSLY
DISCERN	VANQUISHED	PARAPETS	CONSPIRING	OBLIGED

Bridge to Terabithia Vocabulary

SANCTUARY	REPENTED	HYPOCRIITICAL	SOLEMN	ACCUSATION
VIGOROUSLY	DESPISING	SHEBANG	PUDGY	MOURNING
COMMEND	RELENTLESSLY	FREE SPACE	DREDGING	SPORADICALLY
COMPLACENT	CONSTRICTING	PANDEMONIUM	FOUNDLING	DREGS
PROVERBIAL	INSUFFICIENCIES	DOUSED	CAGEY	PREDATORS

Bridge to Terabithia Vocabulary

COMPLACENT	HYPOCRIITICAL	ALCOVE	PANDEMONIUM	CONSTRICTING
OMINOUSLY	DESPITE	VANQUISHED	DELIBERATELY	VILE
CRIMSON	DISCERN	FREE SPACE	FOUNDLING	INSUFFICIENCIES
DREGS	FALTERED	REPENTED	REGICIDE	RELENTLESSLY
COMMEND	MOURNING	SOLEMN	DREAD	PARAPETS

Bridge to Terabithia Vocabulary

CONSOLIDATED	DREDGING	SPECULATION	DESPISING	DELICATELY
DOUSED	GRIT	SPORADICALLY	REGALLY	PREDATORS
RETRIEVED	EXHILARATION	FREE SPACE	SANCTUARY	GARISH
INCLINED	INTOXICATED	PARAMEDICS	PROVERBIAL	ACCUSATION
CONSPIRING	CONSOLATION	RELUCTANT	REVENGE	MUDDLED

Bridge to Terabithia Vocabulary

PUDGY	OBLIGED	ACCUSATION	DESPISING	GRIT
DELICATELY	COMPLACENT	PITEOUSLY	PREDATORS	ALCOVE
MUDDLED	FALTERED	FREE SPACE	SPECULATION	CONSOLIDATED
OMINOUSLY	SPORADICALLY	INSUFFICIENCIES	INTOXICATED	COMMEND
SURPLUS	RETRIEVED	DISCERN	CRIMSON	CONSTRICTING

Bridge to Terabithia Vocabulary

DOUSED	RELUCTANT	EXHILARATION	INCLINED	MOURNING
RELENTLESSLY	REVENGE	NAUSEATINGLY	PARAPETS	REGALLY
DELIBERATELY	DREGS	FREE SPACE	DREDGING	VANQUISHED
PRESCRIBED	SOLEMN	VIGOROUSLY	DESPITE	CONSOLATION
SHEBANG	REPENTED	HYPOCRIITICAL	CAGEY	SPECTACLE

www.ingramcontent.com/pod-product-compliance
Lightning Source LLC
Chambersburg PA
CBHW081454070526
44586CB00019B/2347